Coaching the 3-5-3 Defense

Thomas Cousins

ISBN: 978-1-58518-027-1
Library of Congress Control Number: 2007922047

Book layout and cover design: Jeff Higgerson

Coaches Choice
P.O. Box 1828
Monterey, CA 93942
www.coacheschoice.com

Dedication

For my wife, Danna, and my children, Jeffrey and Haley,
who have always been my biggest supporters, critics, and fans.

For my mom, Darlene, who instilled a
love of reading in me that endures to this day.

For my dad, Howard, who shows me every
day that hard work and determination pay off.

Acknowledgments

Thanks to my assistant coaches, who helped me in producing this book:

- Reginald Knighten
- Jermaine Wilson
- Randolph Monday

Thanks to Bobby Carlton, James Gaskins, Leonard Covington, and Jimbo Walker for influencing my life more than they will ever know.

Thanks to Gary Smallen and Jon Eder, who took a chance on me in college.

Thanks to Fred Hamilton and Doug Miller for teaching me everything I know about this game.

Very special thanks to Dr. James Peterson, who gave me the opportunity to write this book, and to Nate Sassaman, who made it all possible.

Contents

Dedication. 3

Acknowledgments 4

Preface 6

Chapter 1: Overview 7

Chapter 2: Fronts and Line Calls. 17

Chapter 3: Pressure Package. 24

Chapter 4: Coverage Package 74

Chapter 5: Defensive Line Play. 87

Chapter 6: Inside Linebacker Play 103

Chapter 7: Outside Linebacker Play 118

Chapter 8: Defensive Backs Play 127

Chapter 9: Defending Against Power Formations, Power Runs, and the Option . 147

Chapter 10: Defending Against the Spread Offense. 189

Chapter 11: Defending Against Common Plays 208

Chapter 12: Goal-Line Package and Defensive Special Teams 217

Appendix A: Defensive Practice Schedule 231

Apendix B: Installation Schedule. 233

About the Author 234

Preface

This book will teach you how to install and run the entire 3-5-3 defensive package. This defensive scheme has been purposely morphed into a very simple, easy-to-use system that allows for the use of smaller, speed-type players. This book presents all of the tools and resources that any coach needs to be successful in the 3-5-3 defense. Its content will enable any football coach to learn, understand, and teach the entire package through the use of easy-to-understand terminology, easy-to-read illustrations, and everyday language. Included in this book are detailed practice drills for all players in the scheme. All coverages and adjustments are included, as is a very detailed look at the pressure/stunt portion of the package.

We have all been taught as football coaches that offense wins games, but defense wins championships. I honestly believe this statement is true, and because of the 3-5-3 defense I feel that football is becoming more even in terms of matching up with today's high-powered offenses. This defensive concept is not new. The 3-5-3 and all of its variations have been around for years, but because of a few coaches who were willing to "think outside the box," this defensive scheme has become, in my opinion, the great equalizer in terms of matching up smaller, speed-type personnel with both wide-open and power offenses.

Part of the reason I have had success with this defense is the way I approach practice. We are live everyday—no pads, no dummies, and no shorts—Monday through Thursday. I stress everything being full speed in defensive practice so that the players get accustomed to the speed of the game from day one. Another interesting fact is that I have never done pursuit drills in practice. I incorporate them into every drill my team uses in practice; whether it is in individual, inside, skelly, or team drill. Because we are always stressing pursuit, I feel that our kids believe that no other acceptable way exists to practice—only live and full speed.

For you to be successful with this defense, I encourage you to be as open-minded as possible. Many of the techniques and schemes go against what you may have learned as "sound" football. Be creative and be willing to "think outside the box" and you will find that this defense is easy to run and fun for your players. You cannot be bound by what you perceive as boundaries in defensive football. Sure, voiding zones all over the field and having a three-man front on the goal line are not normally considered examples of sound judgment in football, but if you are willing to be a little different and be creative, this defense will work for you as it has for us.

1

Overview

Rationale Behind the 3-5-3 Defense

Consider the following reasons for running the 3-5-3:

- You have few defensive linemen. Finding a 5'11", 220-pound kid is much easier than finding a 6'3", 280-pound player every year.
- You have a bunch of linebacker/strong safety–type players. Every program seems to have an overabundance of these kids.
- You want to get more speed on the field. The great equalizer is speed.
- You have trouble with contain. Contain in the 4-3 can be a bit problematic, but with the 3-5-3 you have leverage players outside on every play.
- You want your players to have fewer coverages to learn. What is better, being 50 percent at 20 coverages or being 100 percent at five or six?
- You want easier linebacker reads for your players. Having players only playing to the strongside or the weakside reduces the amount of linebacker reads they must learn.
- You want to be balanced on both sides of the ball so that adjustments are easy to make against multiple formations. Because the defense is balanced on both sides, usually only one or two people need to adjust to anything they see.

- You want to show an eight-man front, yet still be strong against the pass. The emergence of the spread offense causes most defenses to remove linebackers from the box to cover receivers, which in turn causes a loss of gap integrity.
- You want to find homes for players who in other systems would not have a place to play. Every player who comes out for the team wants to play. Due to the fact that this defense allows for the use of smaller, speed-type players, it can help you find homes for some players who would not otherwise have a spot.

The 3-5-3 defensive has the following advantages:

- Not many coaches seem to know how to block or game plan for the 3-5-3, due to the fact that this defense is not widely used and that most of the defensive reads and reactions are backward from what offenses expect.
- It is extremely flexible. Nickel and dime substitutions can be made without disrupting the overall scheme. In fact, with the right personnel, no substitutions need to be made at all.
- The defense is an eight-man front, yet five speed players are on the field for pass coverage. You get the best of both worlds: pressure and pass defense. As you know, a big difference exists between a defensive end that runs a 5.0 40-yard dash chasing the quarterback and an outside linebacker who runs a 4.5.
- It allows for the use of smaller, speed-type players.
- Offenses do not know where pressure is coming from.
- It is confusing to offensive linemen.

The 3-5-3 does have some perceived disadvantages, including the following:

- Teams lining up and trying to mash your three defensive linemen
- Not covering the tight end
- Not having the ability to get into a coverage other than cover 3 or man
- Not giving multiple looks up front

Consider the following keys to success in the 3-5-3 defense:

- *Pressure*—The use of many different pressures is the biggest key in this defense. You want to keep offenses off-balance and wondering what the defense will do next. Sending pressure from different positions and from different areas of the field will allow the defense to stay one step ahead of the offense. You cannot stay in the base defense without sending someone and expect to be successful in this defense. Everything is predicated on causing the disruption of offensive schemes through pressure.

- *Surge*—The defense will need a surge up the field by the defensive linemen while linebackers create a new line of scrimmage one yard up the field.
- *Game plans*—Take away what they do best. You want to dictate what the offense runs, not let them dictate what you can and cannot do.
- *Offensive coaches*—Make them waste valuable time in practice covering many blitzes and stunts.
- *Divide*—Keep receivers out of the middle of the field with the inside linebackers.
- *Creativity*—Be willing to think "outside the box." Do not be bound by what you have learned to be sound football practices.
- *The quarterback*—Force him to throw off-balance and in a hurry. Keep him guessing about where pressure will be coming. Force the quarterback to lose confidence in his offensive linemen.
- *Running backs*—Pursue relentlessly and wear them down by gang tackling. Make the running back not want to carry the ball.
- *Receivers*—Never let a receiver cross a defender's face without being hit. Pretty soon, they will be more worried about getting hit than catching the ball.
- *Offensive linemen*—Keep them in a state of confusion. They never know where a stunt or blitz will be coming from. Make all five offensive linemen have to account for your three defensive linemen.

The success of the 3-5-3 defensive scheme is largely predicated on the use of pressure to disrupt blocking schemes and keep the offense in a state of confusion. Pressure can be achieved by either line slants or by one-, two-, three-, four-, or five-man blitzes.

Pressure is the great equalizer in terms of personnel mismatches in speed, size, or a combination of both. To achieve success with this defense, the concept of pressure needs to be understood and mastered.

Defensive Theory

The players in this system must be convinced that they are the playmakers on the field. The old saying, "bend but don't break," simply does not fit this defensive scheme, which is a big-play defense. Sacks, take-aways, tackles for losses, and caused fumbles all lead to changes in momentum. The job of the defense is to erode the confidence of the offense and make them start second-guessing their scheme, game plan, and coaches. When this doubt takes shape, the defense is dictating the tone of the game and the offense is playing catch-up. No matter what happens during the course of a game, it is the defense that must dictate to the offense what plays can or cannot be run.

Redundancy

One of the strengths of this defensive scheme is that it has redundancy built in for almost every situation. More than one person is usually assigned to do the same job. For example, if the primary force player, the Stud, falls down during the play, the corner is assigned secondary force so that the defense will still accomplish what it set out to do. Examples of redundancy include the following:

- Having both the outside linebackers and the corners assigned to force
- Having both the outside linebacker and the corners assigned to pitch on the option
- Having refit reads for the inside linebackers
- Having the free safety assigned to run the alley for secondary run support

Personnel

Two schools of thought exist when dealing with personnel and personnel groupings. Either flip sides with your defense, creating a strongside and a weakside, or have a right side and a left side that do not flip. For simplicity, this defense is designed to flip sides to keep the players from having to learn multiple reads.

In the 3-5-3 system, the outside linebackers are called Stud (strong) and Whip (weak). As the keys to this defense, they are hybrids that cannot only defeat the block of the tight end or fullback, but also cover man-to-man if needed. To be even more position-specific, the Stud can be more of a true linebacker and the Whip can be more of a true defensive back. These two players will line up four yards deep and four yards outside the end man on the line of scrimmage, but they will have total freedom of movement anywhere in their areas of play, unless dictated to adjust by formations.

The inside linebackers are called Sam (strong) and Will (weak). They line up behind the tackles three-and-a-half to four yards deep. They also have total freedom of movement anywhere in their areas of play. They need to move back and forth and side-to-side to confuse the offense about whether they are blitzing or not. They do not need to be overly big players, but they must be able to run.

The Mike linebacker will line up behind the nose three-and-a-half to four yards deep. He also will have total freedom of movement anywhere in his area of play. He needs to move back and forth and side to side to confuse the offense about whether he is blitzing or not. He needs to be your toughest, most physical linebacker. He can be a step slower than the other two inside linebackers.

The defensive line consists of two tackles that typically align head up to the offensive tackles. Quickness, not strength, is most important. The defensive linemen are never asked to take on the player across from them man-to-man, so they can be smaller than in other systems. The noseguard will line up head up to the center. He needs to be the best defensive lineman on the field and he must command a double-team. The defensive linemen will line up as close to the ball as possible. It is paramount that the five offensive linemen are forced to account for the three defensive linemen.

The free safety must be able to run the alley and also be effective in the passing game. He will be counted on to be active in the running game, so he must be willing to come up and make a tackle. If you have a corner that is a good tackler but a step too slow to be an every-down cover guy, then he may be able to play free safety.

The corners are simply the best athletes on the field. They will be left on an island quite a bit, so they must be cover players with good instincts. In regards to the running game, the corners will be asked to provide secondary support and take the pitchback late on the option.

Gaps

This defense uses a pretty standard gap numbering system. It is important that the players know and understand techniques and gaps as they relate to where everyone fits in a particular play. Each individual gap starts at the nose of the inside man and extends to the nose of the next man to the outside (Figure 1-1).

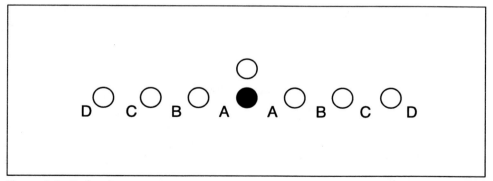

Figure 1-1. Defensive gaps

Techniques

Once again, this defense uses a fairly common numbering system to define individual techniques on players. Figure 1-2 depicts the technique numbering system that is used throughout this book.

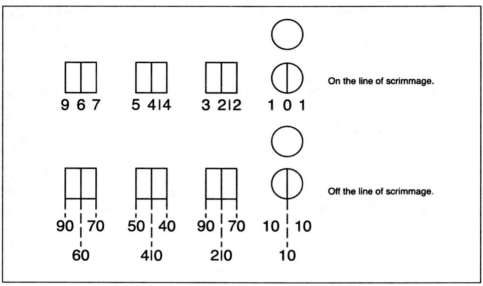

Figure 1-2. Defensive techniques

Huddle

The arrangement of the defensive huddle is very important to the overall scheme, simply because you need to be assured that everyone hears the line call, blitz, and coverage. After the huddle is broken, it is important for the defensive players to remain clustered in the middle of the field and close to the ball until the strength call is made (Figure 1-3).

Defensive Signals

The signals for calling this defense involve a coach using both hands and making gestures or touching various parts of the body. The following lists present defensive signals regarding fronts, line calls, positions, pressures, coverages, and other miscellaneous situations.

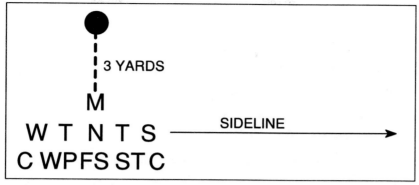

Figure 1-3. Defensive huddle

Fronts

- Base—no signal is given
- Jet—hold both arms out to the side like the wings of an airplane
- Tuff—beat on the chest with both hands like a gorilla
- Goal line—place both hands on the shoulders

Line Calls

- Slant—use the right arm to make a slash in front of the body from top right to bottom left
- Strong—hold the right arm up as when flexing the biceps
- Weak—hold the right arm down, making a 90-degree angle with the elbow
- In—make an inward gesture in front of the body with both hands
- Out—make an outward gesture in front of the body with both hands
- Pinch—make a pinching gesture with the right hand on the right hip (love handle)

Positions

- Sam—tap on the chest with the right fist
- Will—form a W with three fingers of the right hand and tap on the chest
- Mike—touch the stomach with the right hand
- Stud—touch the right thigh with the right hand
- Whip—touch the left thigh with the left hand

Pressures

- Go—form a fist with the right hand and punch outward from the chest
- A—form an A with both hands in front of the body
- Fire—use the right hand to make a gesture like shooting a gun
- Bat—flap both hands in front of the chest
- Dog—place the index fingers on top of the head to form dog ears
- Smash—punch the right hand downward into the left palm
- Wash—make an upside down W with three fingers of the right hand and wave it in front of the body

Coverages

- Cover 3—hold three fingers overhead
- Cover man—tap on top of the head
- Cover 1—hold one finger overhead
- Cover 4—hold the fist up overhead
- Sky—push the palm of the right hand upward toward the sky

Other Signals

- Spy—act as if holding binoculars to the eyes
- Time-out after next play—hold a time-out signal upside down in front of the body
- Run the same thing again—roll both hands forward in front of the body

Sample Defensive Signal Call

An example of a complete defensive signal call is as follows. To call "slant strong, Mike go, Whip fire," the signals would be:

- Make a slash in front of the body with the right arm from top right to bottom left.
- Hold the right arm up as when flexing a muscle.
- Touch the stomach with the right hand.
- Form a fist with the right hand and punch outward from the chest.
- Touch the left thigh with the left hand.
- Use the right hand to make a gesture like shooting a gun.

This process sounds complicated, but it is actually very easy to learn. Some of the longer calls can be put on a wristband. Everything else can be signaled in from the sideline.

Play-Calling Procedure

In the huddle, the Mike linebacker will receive the signal from the coach on the sideline. After he has the signal, Mike will repeat twice to the other defensive players what was signaled in. Mike may say something such as, "Slant strong, mike go, cover 3; slant strong, mike go, cover 3."

Mike will then yell "GA" and the rest of the defense will yell back "TA" while clapping their hands at the same time. G.A.T.A stands for "get after them aggressively," which is the battle cry of this defense.

Strength Call

The first thing that needs to be done once the huddle has been broken is to declare the strength side. The Mike linebacker will have the responsibility to recognize and declare the strength side.

- The strength is determined first by the tight end (Figure 1-4).
- If no tight end is involved, then the call is made to the multiple-receiver side (Figure 1-5).

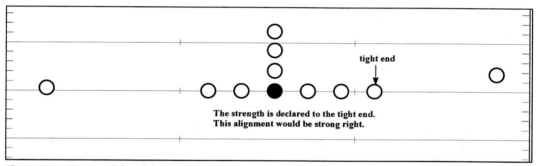

Figure 1-4. Strong right, tight end

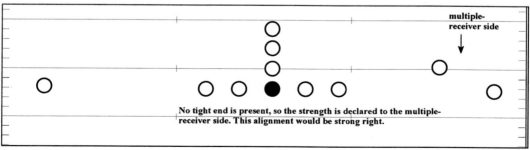

Figure 1-5. Strong right, multiple receivers

- If the formation is balanced and on a hash, the strength call will be made to the field (Figure 1-6).
- If the formation is balanced and in the middle of the field, the strength call will be made to the left (due to the fact that most quarterbacks are right-handed) (Figure 1-7).

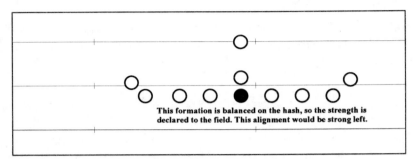

This formation is balanced on the hash, so the strength is declared to the field. This alignment would be strong left.

Figure 1-6. Strong left, field

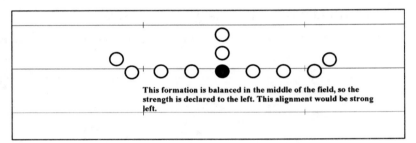

This formation is balanced in the middle of the field, so the strength is declared to the left. This alignment would be strong left.

Figure 1-7. Strong left

Through game-planning, times will arise when you may want to declare the strength always to the field or even to the right or left as the offense's tendencies dictate. This adjustment should be made if a team runs predominantly to the field, or to their right or left.

2

Fronts and Line Calls

The 3-5-3 defense uses only four different fronts. The base front is a three-man front, which will be used approximately 95 percent of the time. The other three fronts are very situation-specific. Tuff is used to jam the tight end, jet is used only in passing situations while paired with a prevent coverage, and goal line is used in short-yardage and goal-line situations.

Fronts

Base Front

This front does not have a name; it is the base call in this defense. The nose is in a 0 technique, head up to the center and as close to the ball as possible. The tackles are in 4i techniques, head up to the tackles and as close to the ball as possible. The Mike linebacker is in a 00 technique, stacked behind the nose three-and-a-half to four yards deep. Sam and Will are stacked behind the defensive tackles in 40i techniques, three-and-a-half to four yards deep. The outside linebackers (Stud and Whip) are four yards outside the end man on the line of scrimmage and three-and-a-half to four yards deep, unless dictated to align otherwise due to a formation adjustment. The defensive backs will be aligned as dictated by the coverage call (Figure 2-1).

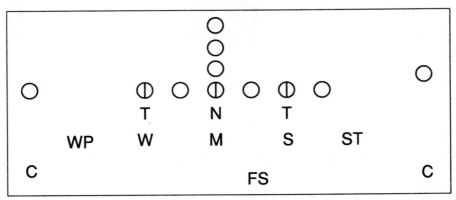

Figure 2-1. The base front

Tuff

The tuff front is used to jam the tight end. The nose is in a 0 technique, head up to the center and as close to the ball as possible. The tackles are in 4i techniques, head up to the tackles and as close to the ball as possible. The Mike linebacker is in a 00 technique over the center and three-and-a-half to four yards deep. Sam and Will are stacked behind the defensive tackles in 40i techniques and three-and-a-half to four yards deep. The Whip linebacker is four yards outside the end man on the line of scrimmage and three-and-a-half to four yards deep, unless dictated to align otherwise due to a formation adjustment. The Stud linebacker will walk up and play a loose 9 technique on the tight end. He will engage the tight end only if the tight end blocks down or attempts to free release up the field. The Stud will jam the tight end and redirect his path. The Stud will then run the tight end's feet into the backfield, looking for a trap or kick-out. The defensive backs will be aligned as dictated by the coverage call (Figure 2-2).

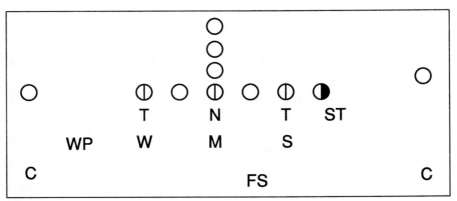

Figure 2-2. The tuff front

Jet

The jet front is only used in obvious passing situations. The nose is in a 0 technique, head up to the center and as close to the ball as possible. The strong tackle is in a loose 9 technique outside the tight end and as close to the ball as possible. The weak tackle is in a loose 5 technique outside the offensive tackle and as close to the ball as possible. The Mike linebacker is in a 00 technique over the center and three-and-a-half to four yards deep. Sam and Will are stacked behind the defensive tackles in 40i techniques and three-and-a-half to four yards deep. The outside linebackers (Stud and Whip) are three-and-a-half to four yards deep and four yards outside the end man on the line of scrimmage, unless dictated to align otherwise due to a formation adjustment. The defensive backs will be aligned as dictated by the coverage call (Figure 2-3).

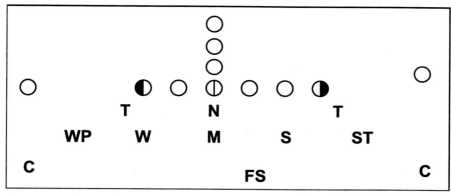

Figure 2-3. The jet front

Goal Line

The goal-line front is used in short-yardage and goal-line situations. The nose is in a 0 technique, head up to the center and as close to the ball as possible. The tackles are in 4 techniques, inside the shoulder of the offensive tackles and as close to the ball as possible. The Mike linebacker is in a 00 technique over the center and three-and-a-half to four yards deep. Sam and Will are stacked behind the defensive tackles in 40i techniques and three-and-a-half to four yards deep. The outside linebackers (Stud and Whip) are both walked up off the end man on the line of scrimmage. The Whip will be in a loose 5 technique on the offensive tackle and the Stud will be in a loose 9 technique on the tight end. In the case of a double-tight-end formation, the Whip will bump to a loose 9 on the weak tight end. The defensive backs will be aligned as dictated by the coverage call (Figure 2-4).

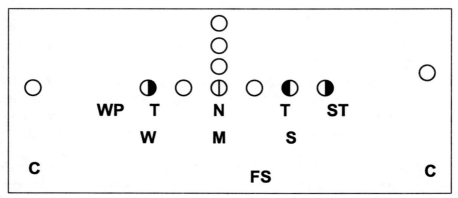

Figure 2-4. The goal-line front

Adjustments
Base Vs. Double Tight Ends (Figure 2-5)

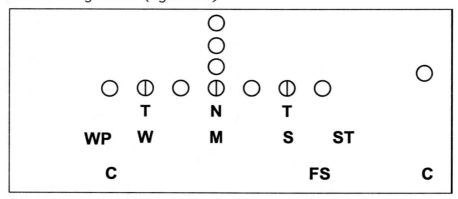

Figure 2-5. Stud and Whip will tighten up to two yards wide by four yards deep.

Base Vs. Unbalanced (Figure 2-6)

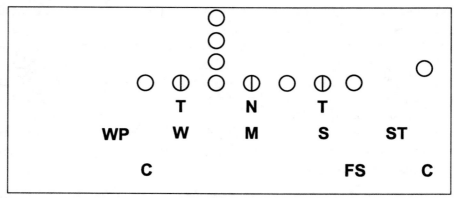

Figure 2-6. Bump the entire defensive front one whole man toward the offensive strength.

Base Vs. Overload (Figure 2-7)

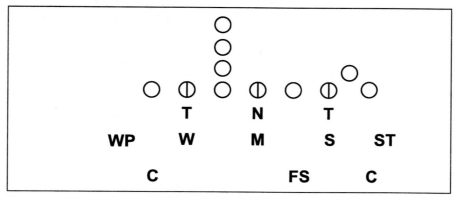

Figure 2-7. Bump the entire front; Stud must be aligned head up to or outside of the end man.

Line Calls

On every defensive play they run, the defensive linemen will perform one of five line calls. The defensive linemen will be moving on every play. They will never be asked to take on the offensive lineman they are lined up over, which is why the defensive linemen can be smaller than they would be in other defensive systems.

Slant Strong

The first line call this defense will use is slant strong. In slant strong, the defensive linemen will be slanting toward the strength call. The strong tackle will perform a crossover step, dip and rip, and get to the hip of the tight end to his side. The weak tackle will perform a crossover step, dip and rip, and get to the hip of the weak guard. The nose will perform a crossover step, dip and rip, and get to the hip of the strong guard (Figure 2-8).

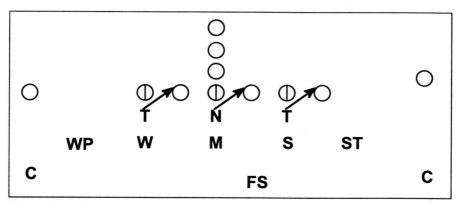

Figure 2-8. Slant strong

Slant Weak

The next line call this defense will use is slant weak. In slant weak, the defensive linemen will be slanting away from the strength call as dictated in Chapter 1. The strong tackle will perform a crossover step, dip and rip, and get to the hip of the strong guard. The weak tackle will perform a crossover step, dip and rip, and get to the hip of the tight end to his side (if no tight end is present, he gets to the hip of an imaginary tight end). The nose will perform a crossover step, dip and rip, and get to the hip of the weak guard (Figure 2-9).

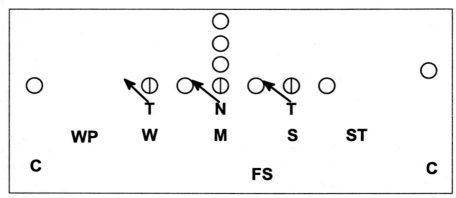

Figure 2-9. Slant weak

In

The next line call used is called "in." The defensive tackles will be slanting to the hips of both guards. Both tackles will perform a crossover step, dip and rip, and get to the hip of the guard to his side. The nose will always slant to the strength call. He will perform a crossover step, dip and rip, and get to the hip of the strong guard (Figure 2-10).

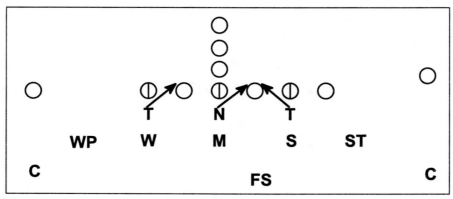

Figure 2-10. In

Out

The next line call used is called "out." The defensive tackles will be slanting to the hips of either tight end (or an imaginary tight end on the weakside). Both tackles will perform a crossover step, dip and rip, and get to the hip of the tight end to his side. The nose will always slant to the strength call. He will perform a crossover step, dip and rip, and get to the hip of the strong guard (Figure 2-11).

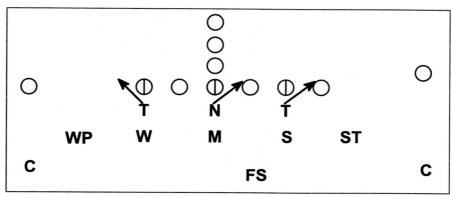

Figure 2-11. Out

Pinch

The last line call used is pinch. The defensive tackles will be slanting to the hips of both guards, just as they would with an in call. Both tackles will perform a crossover step, dip and rip, and get to the hip of the guard to his side. The nose will always slant away from the strength call. He will perform a crossover step, dip and rip, and get to the hip of the weak guard (Figure 2-12).

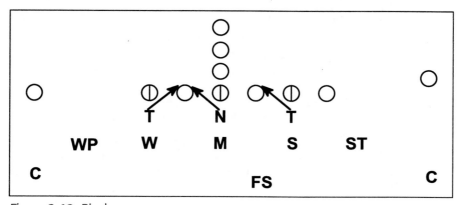

Figure 2-12. Pinch

3

Pressure Package

As stated in Chapter 1, the use of pressure is the key element of success in the 3-5-3 defense. Pressure on the offense can be produced in many ways. Through the use of a very simple terminology system, you can tag one player or up to six people to blitz. The defensive line is always slanting one way or the other, so you can simply tag a blitz onto the existing line call (Figure 3-1). It is not vital that the linebackers know where the defensive linemen are slanting. The linebackers simply walk up behind the defensive linemen and blitz opposite, or they can hit the blitz on a delay after the defensive lineman has slanted. The linebackers have the freedom to decide how they want to blitz and from what depth. Some of the blitzes in this scheme are packaged to cut down on the length of calls. Some of the longer calls can be put onto a wristband, while everything else will be signaled in from the sideline.

Due to the fact that all you will be doing is tagging blitzes onto a line call, calling one pressure, Sam go for instance, actually turns into several different combinations. Slant strong, Sam go has the tackle slanting into the strong C gap and Sam going to the strong B gap (Figure 3-2). Calling slant weak, Sam go will have the tackle slanting to the strong B gap and Sam going to the strong C gap (Figure 3-3). This blitz can be called with all five of the line calls.

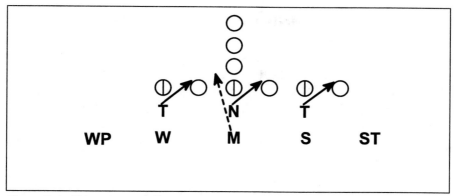

Figure 3-1. Slant strong, Mike go

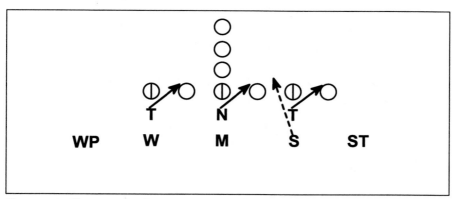

Figure 3-2. Slant strong, Sam go

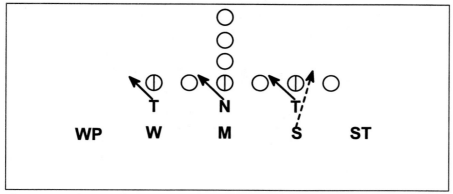

Figure 3-3. Slant weak, Sam go

Play-Calling Procedures

If Whip fire or Stud fire is called, then the Whip or Stud will be blitzing alone. If just fire is called, then both of them will be blitzing. The same can be said for a dog call. If strong dog is called, then the Mike and Sam are blitzing. If weak dog is called, then the Mike and Will are blitzing. If just dog is called, then all three players are blitzing.

Marrying Calls

You must marry some blitzes between the line call and the linebacker movement. This issue is only a concern when making calls that assign a player to blitz a specific gap (e.g., Will A and Stud A). For example, you can't call in, Stud A, because a gap conflict would be created, with two people in the same gap. Instead pinch, Stud A must be called.

Pressure Packages

The following pressure package is divided into five parts. Whenever applicable, each pressure is illustrated with the five line calls used.

Four-Man Pressures

Mike Go (Figures 3-4 through 3-8)

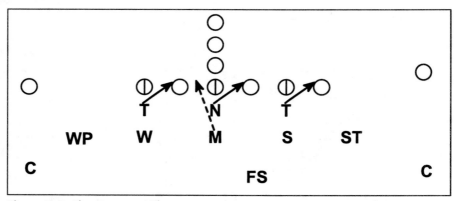

Figure 3-4. Slant strong, Mike go

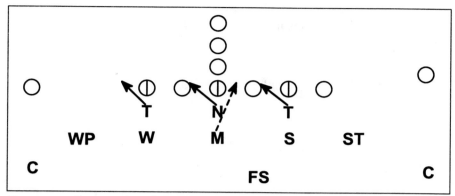

Figure 3-5. Slant weak, Mike go

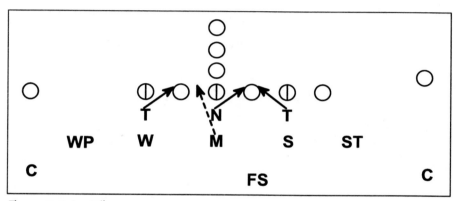

Figure 3-6. In, Mike go

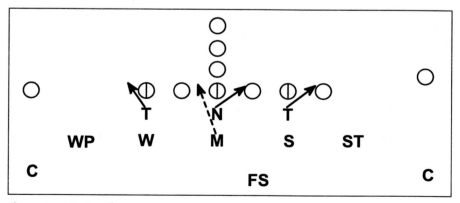

Figure 3-7. Out, Mike go

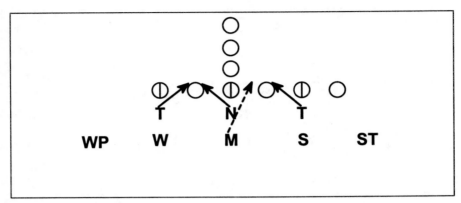

Figure 3-8. Pinch, Mike go

Will Go (Figures 3-9 through 3-13)

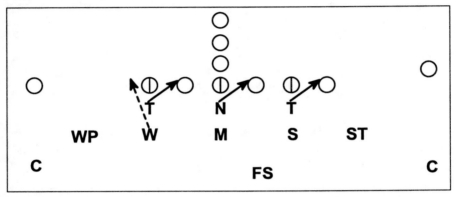

Figure 3-9. Slant strong, Will go

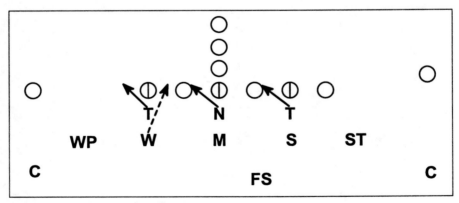

Figure 3-10. Slant weak, Will go

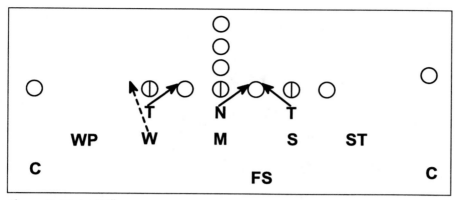

Figure 3-11. In, Will go

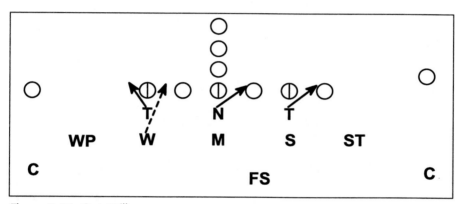

Figure 3-12. Out, Will go

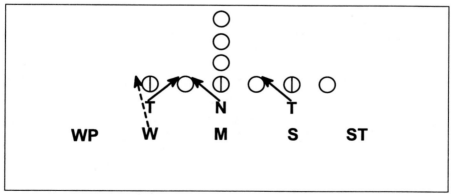

Figure 3-13. Pinch, Will go

Sam Go (Figures 3-14 through 3-18)

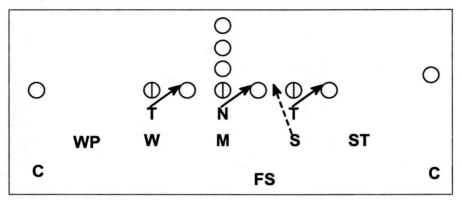

Figure 3-14. Slant strong, Sam go

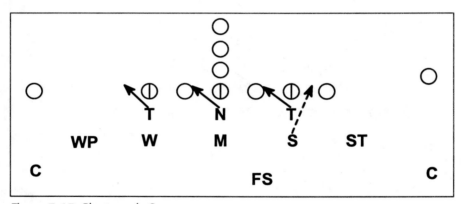

Figure 3-15. Slant weak, Sam go

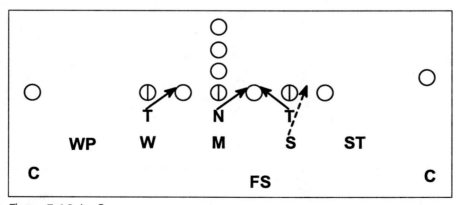

Figure 3-16. In, Sam go

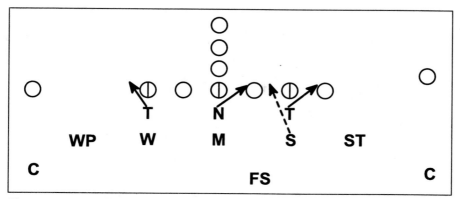

Figure 3-17. Out, Sam go

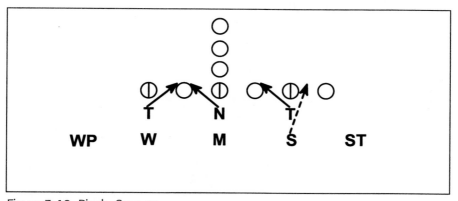

Figure 3-18. Pinch, Sam go

Whip Fire (Figures 3-19 through 3-23)

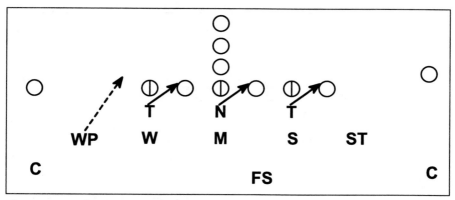

Figure 3-19. Slant strong, Whip fire

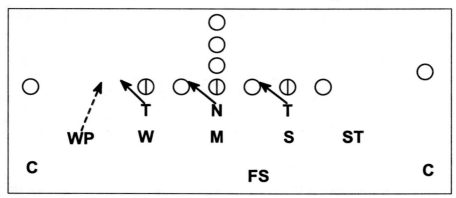

Figure 3-20. Slant weak, Whip fire

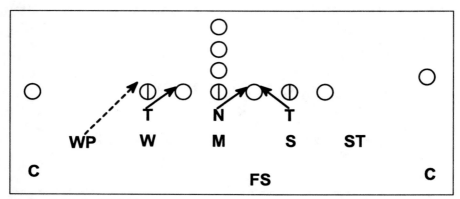

Figure 3-21. In, Whip fire

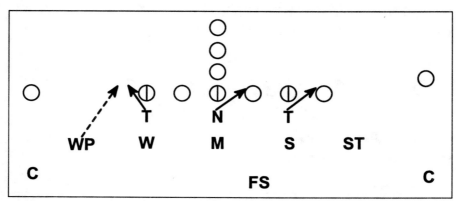

Figure 3-22. Out, Whip fire

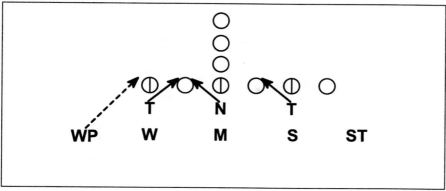

Figure 3-23. Pinch, Whip fire

Stud Fire (Figures 3-24 through 3-28)

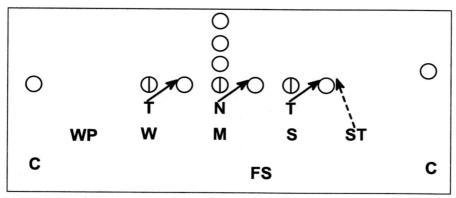

Figure 3-24. Slant strong, Stud fire

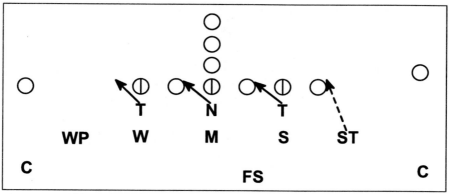

Figure 3-25. Slant weak, Stud fire

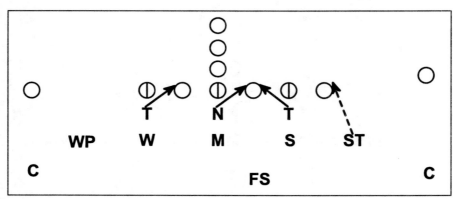

Figure 3-26. In, Stud fire

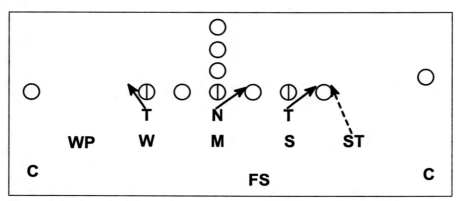

Figure 3-27. Out, Stud fire

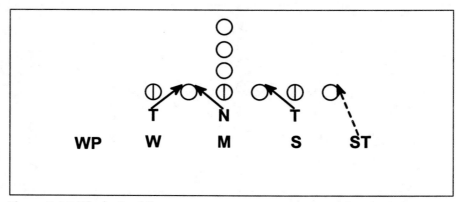

Figure 3-28. Pinch, Stud fire

Sam A (Figures 3-29 and 3-30)

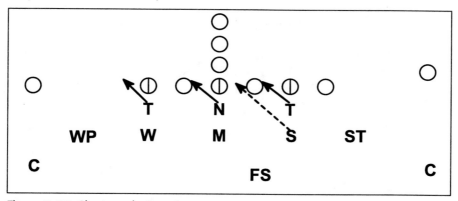

Figure 3-29. Slant weak, Sam A

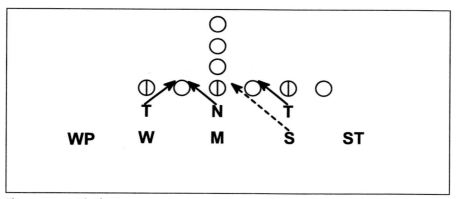

Figure 3-30. Pinch, Sam A

Will A (Figures 3-31 through 3-33)

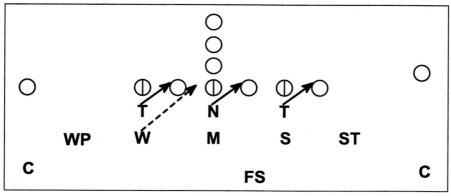

Figure 3-31. Slant strong, Will A

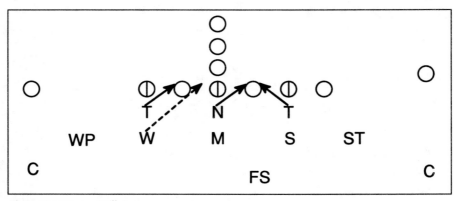

Figure 3-32. In, Will A

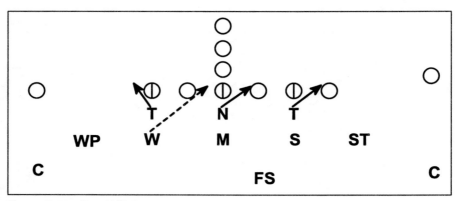

Figure 3-33. Out, Will A

Five-Man Pressures

Bat (Figure 3-34 through 3-38)

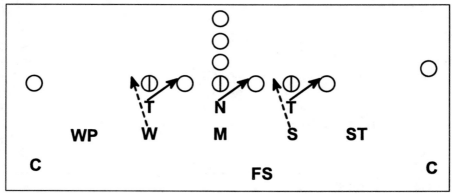

Figure 3-34. Slant strong, bat

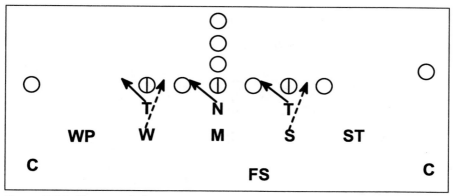

Figure 3-35. Slant weak, bat

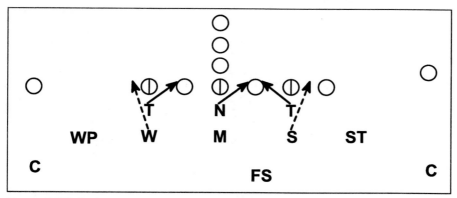

Figure 3-36. In, bat

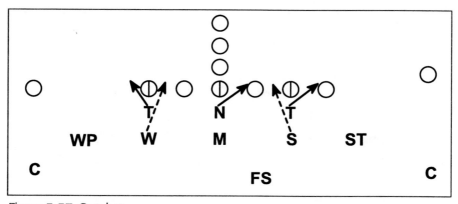

Figure 3-37. Out, bat

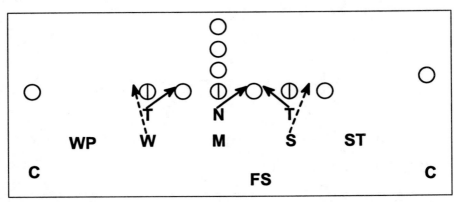

Figure 3-38. bat

Dog Weak (Figures 3-39 through 3-43)

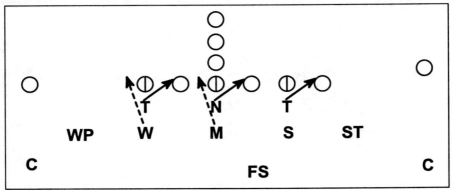

Figure 3-39. Slant strong, dog weak

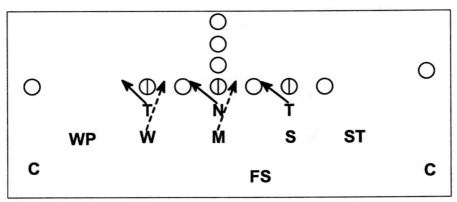

Figure 3-40. Slant weak, dog weak

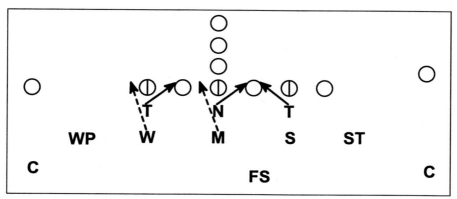

Figure 3-41. In, dog weak

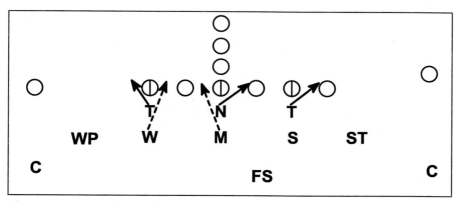

Figure 3-42. Out, dog weak

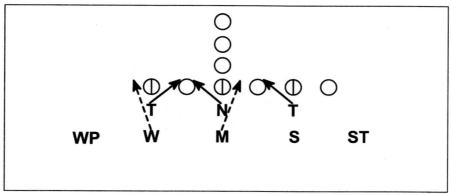

Figure 3-43. Pinch, dog weak

Dog Strong (Figures 3-44 through 3-48)

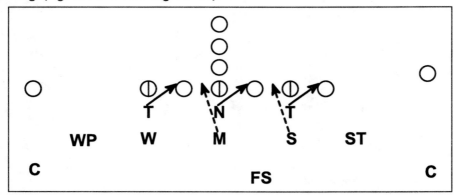

Figure 3-44. Slant strong, dog strong

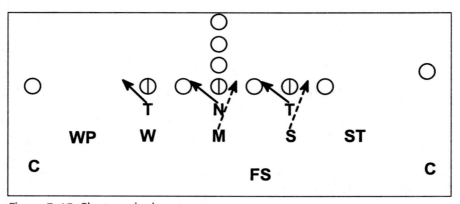

Figure 3-45. Slant weak, dog strong

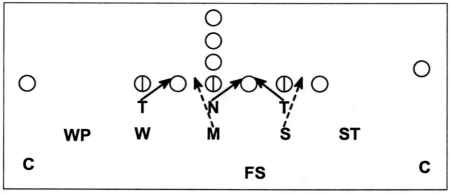

Figure 3-46. In, dog strong

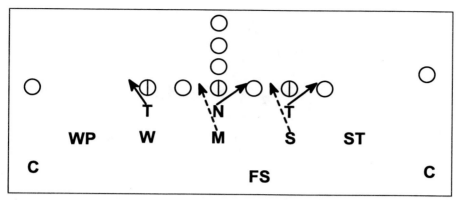

Figure 3-47. Out, dog strong

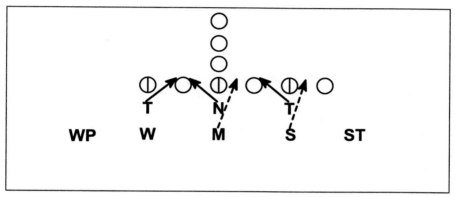

Figure 3-48. Pinch, dog strong

Double A (Figures 3-49 through 3-53)

When double A is called, the nose needs to know that he is not performing the line call; instead he is crabbing the center upfield. The nose will try and put his entire body in the center's way and occupy him for the blitz to clear. Double A is the only time that the line call will deviate from what is called.

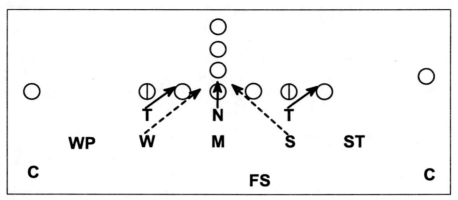

Figure 3-49. Slant strong, double A

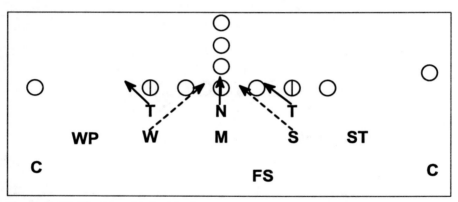

Figure 3-50. Slant weak, double A

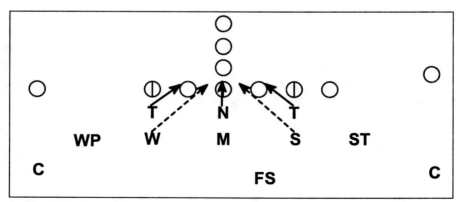

Figure 3-51. In, double A

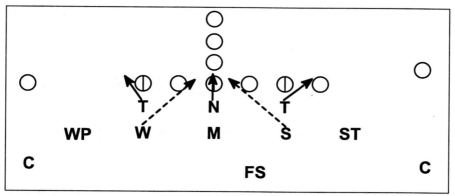

Figure 3-52. Out, double A

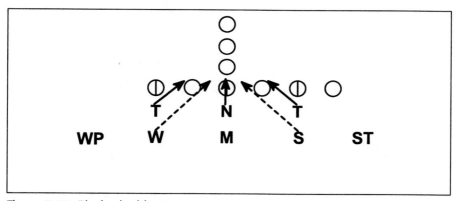

Figure 3-53. Pinch, double A

Fire (Figures 3-54 through 3-58)

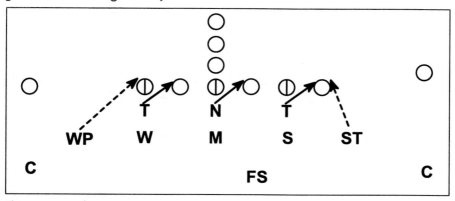

Figure 3-54. Slant strong, fire

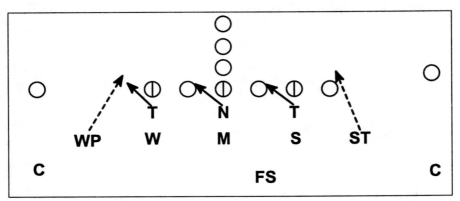

Figure 3-55. Slant weak, fire

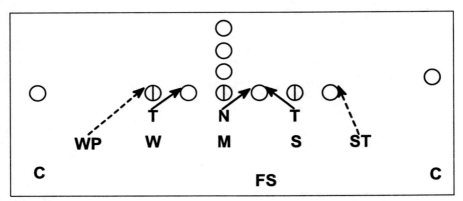

Figure 3-56. In, fire

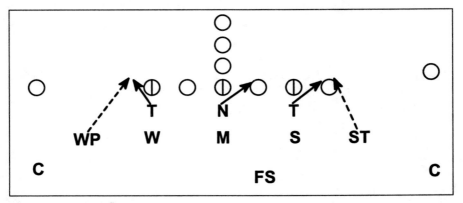

Figure 3-57. Out, fire

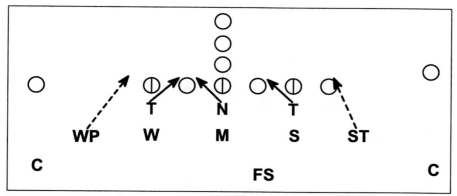

Figure 3-58. Pinch, fire

Smash (Figures 3-59 through 3-63)

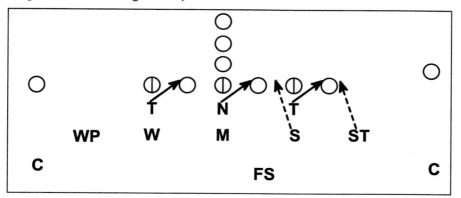

Figure 3-59. Slant strong, smash

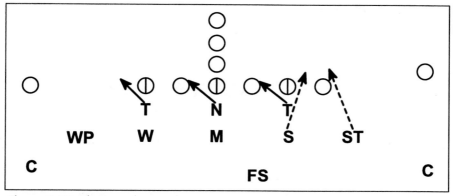

Figure 3-60. Slant weak, smash

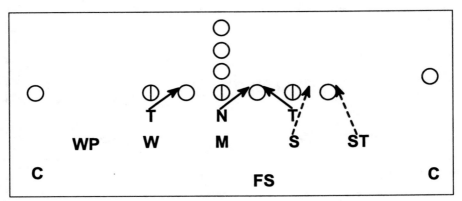

Figure 3-61. In, smash

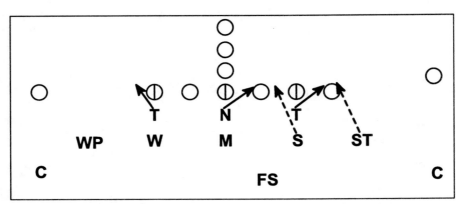

Figure 3-62. Out, smash

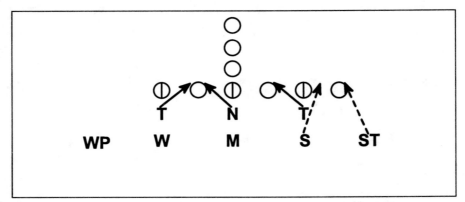

Figure 3-63. Pinch, smash

Wash (Figures 3-64 through 3-68)

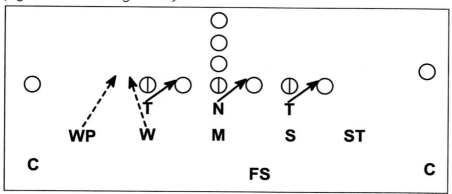

Figure 3-64. Slant strong, wash

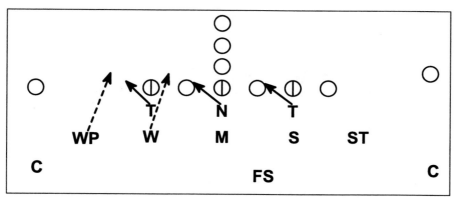

Figure 3-65. Slant weak, wash

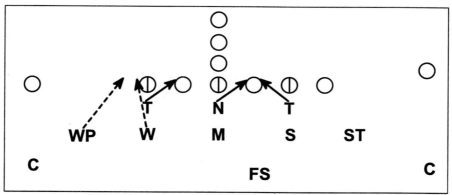

Figure 3-66. In, wash

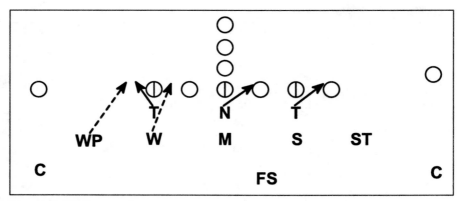

Figure 3-67. Out, wash

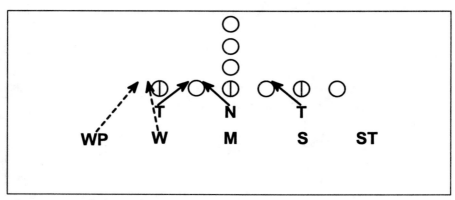

Figure 3-68. Pinch, wash

Mike Go, Stud Fire (Figures 3-69 through 3-73)

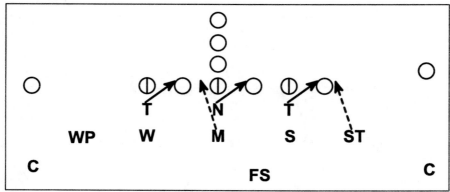

Figure 3-69. Slant strong, Mike go, Stud fire

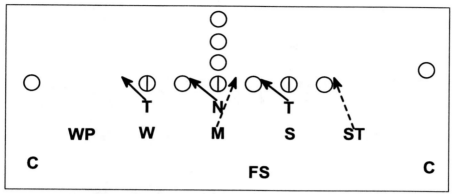

Figure 3-70. Slant weak, Mike go, Stud fire

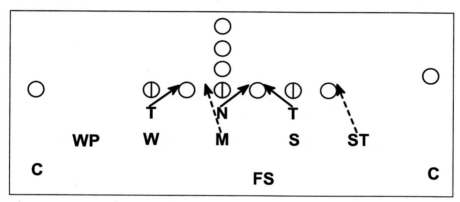

Figure 3-71. In, Mike go, Stud fire

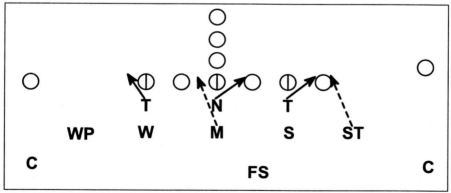

Figure 3-72. Out, Mike go, Stud fire

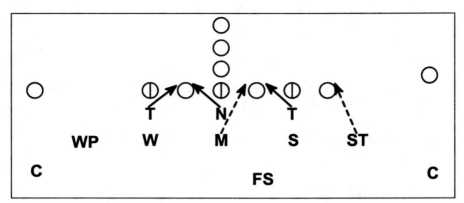

Figure 3-73. Pinch, Mike go, Stud fire

Mike Go, Whip Fire (Figures 3-74 through 3-78)

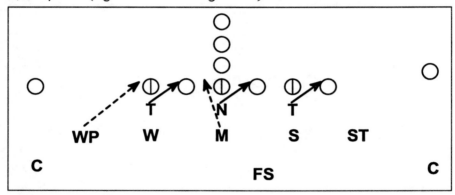

Figure 3-74. Slant strong, Mike go, Whip fire

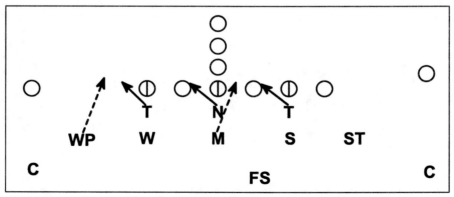

Figure 3-75. Slant weak, Mike go, Whip fire

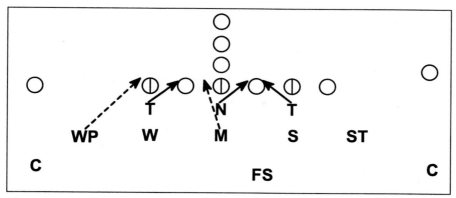

Figure 3-76. In, Mike go, Whip fire

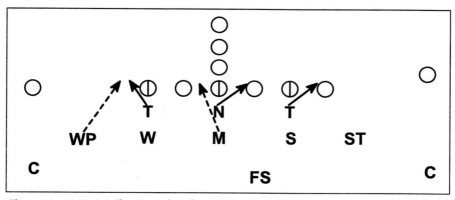

Figure 3-77. Out, Mike go, Whip fire

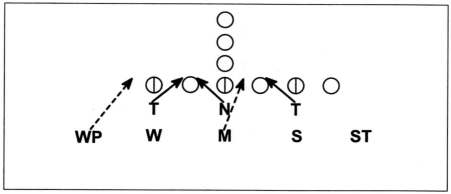

Figure 3-78. Pinch, Mike go, Whip fire

Will Go, Stud Fire (Figures 3-79 through 3-83)

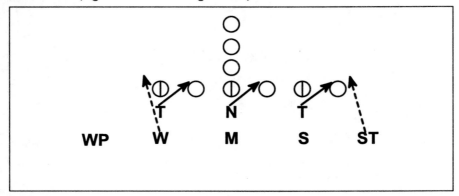

Figure 3-79. Slant strong, Will go, Stud fire

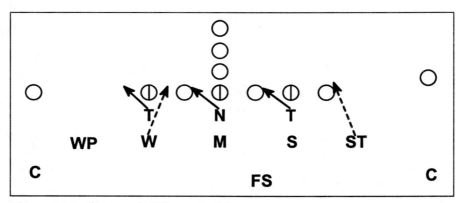

Figure 3-80. Slant weak, Will go, Stud fire

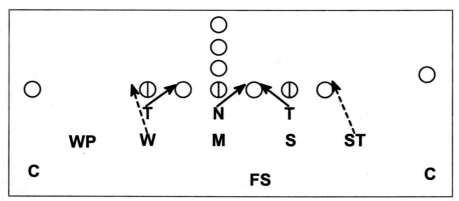

Figure 3-81. In, Will go, Stud fire

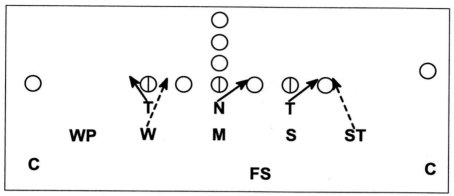

Figure 3-82. Out, Will go, Stud fire

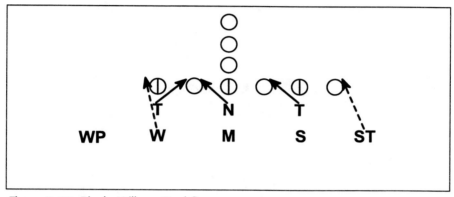

Figure 3-83. Pinch, Will go, Stud fire

Sam Go, Whip Fire (Figures 3-84 through 3-88)

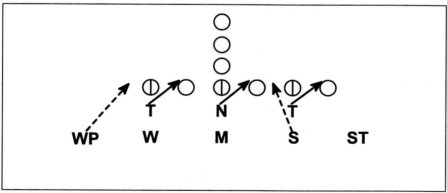

Figure 3-84. Slant strong, Sam go, Whip fire

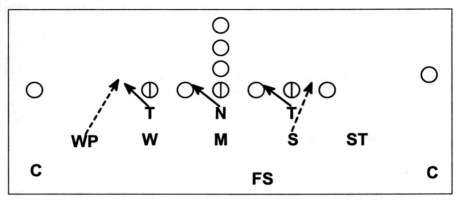

Figure 3-85. Slant weak, Sam go, Whip fire

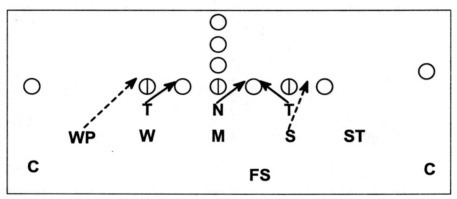

Figure 3-86. In, Sam go, Whip fire

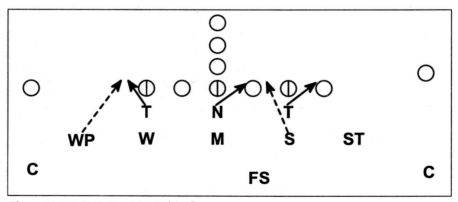

Figure 3-87. Out, Sam go, Whip fire

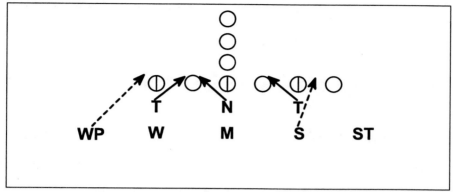

Figure 3-88. Pinch, Sam go, Whip fire

Will A, Whip Fire (Figures 3-89 through 3-91)

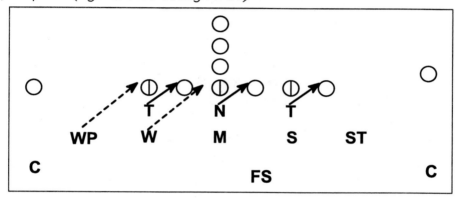

Figure 3-89. Slant strong, Will A, Whip fire

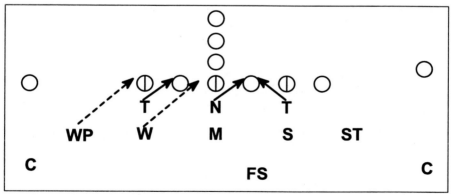

Figure 3-90. In, Will A, Whip fire

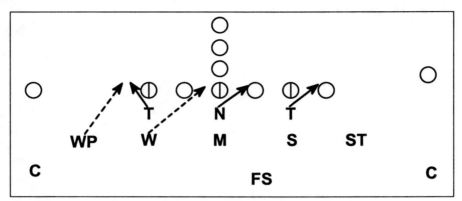

Figure 3-91. Out, Will A, Whip fire

Sam A, Whip Fire (Figures 3-92 and 3-93)

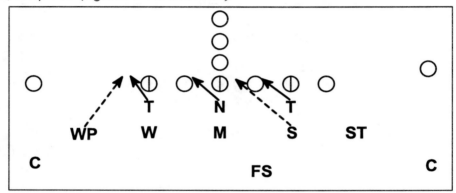

Figure 3-92. Slant weak, Sam A, Whip fire

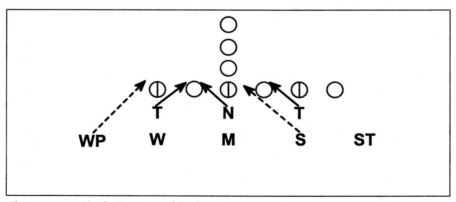

Figure 3-93. Pinch, Sam A, Whip fire

Sam A, Stud Fire (Figures 3-94 and 3-95)

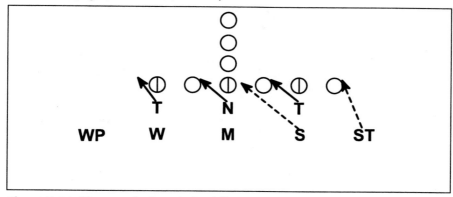

Figure 3-94. Slant weak, Sam A, Stud fire

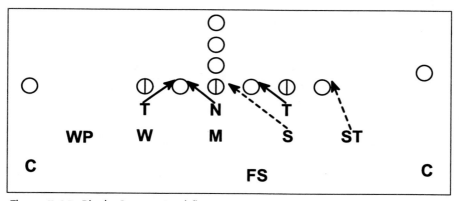

Figure 3-95. Pinch, Sam A, Stud fire

Will A, Sam Go (Figures 3-96 through 3-98)

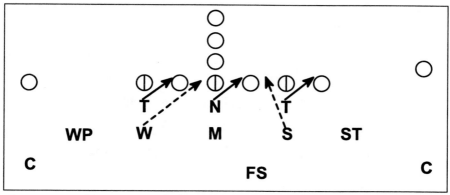

Figure 3-96. Slant strong, Will A, Sam go

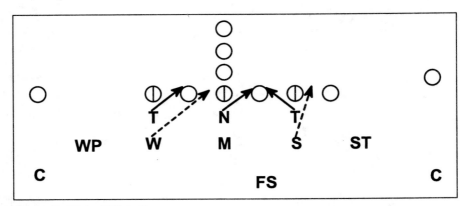

Figure 3-97. In, Will A, Sam go

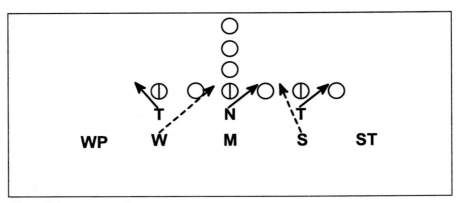

Figure 3-98. Out, Will A, Sam go

Six-Man Pressures

Dog (Figures 3-99 through 3-103)

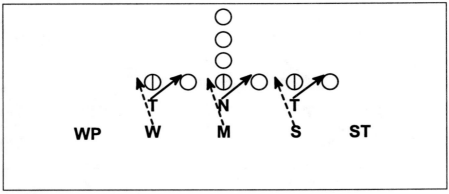

Figure 3-99. Slant strong, dog

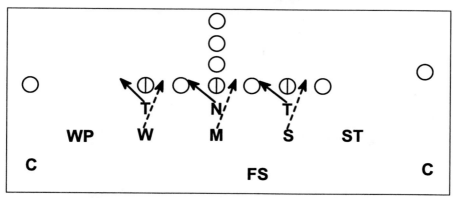

Figure 3-100. Slant weak, dog

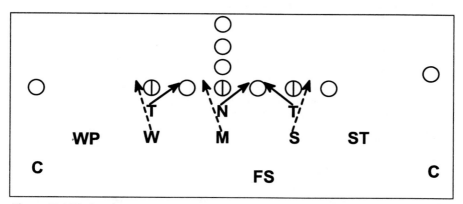

Figure 3-101. In, dog

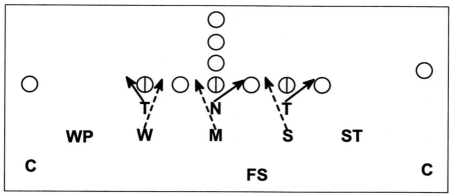

Figure 3-102. Out, dog

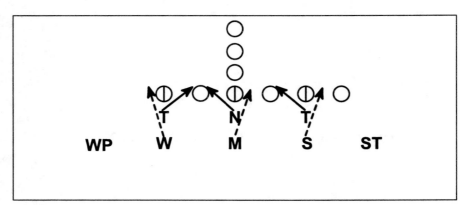

Figure 3-103. Pinch, dog

Smash, Will Go (Figures 3-104 through 3-108)

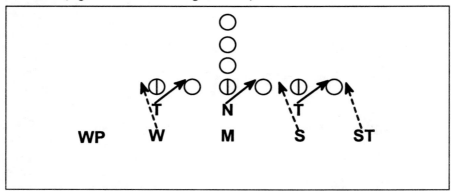

Figure 3-104. Slant strong, smash, Will go

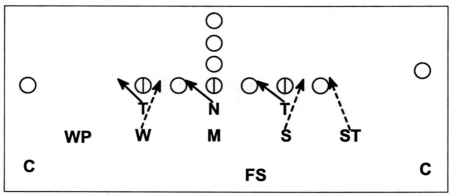

Figure 3-105. Slant weak, smash, Will go

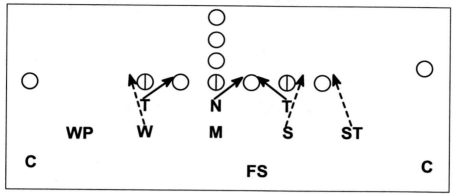

Figure 3-106. In, smash, Will go

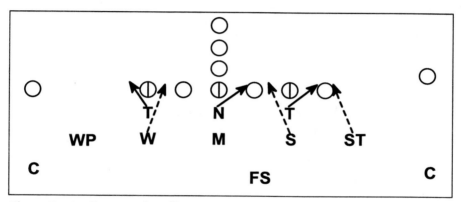

Figure 3-107. Out, smash, Will go

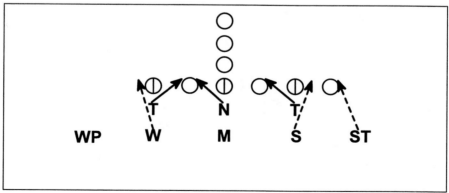

Figure 3-108. Pinch, smash, Will go

Wash, Sam Go (Figures 3-109 through 3-113)

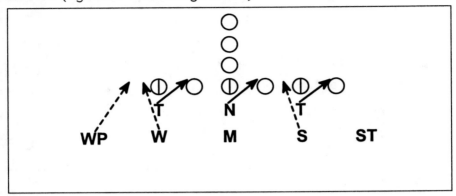

Figure 3-109. Slant strong, wash, Sam go

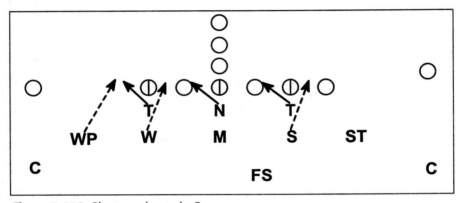

Figure 3-110. Slant weak, wash, Sam go

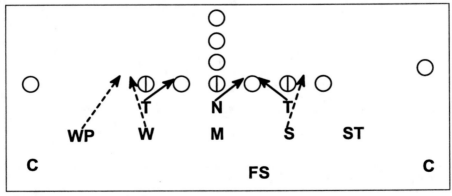

Figure 3-111. In, wash, Sam go

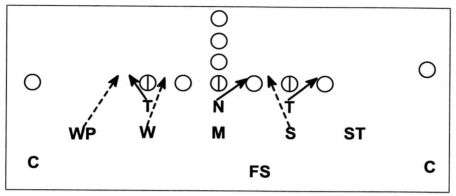

Figure 3-112. Out, wash, Sam go

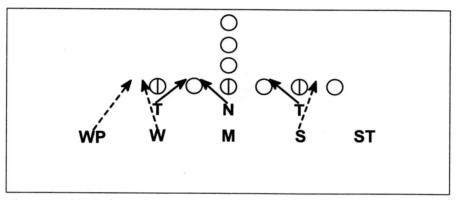

Figure 3-113. Pinch, wash, Sam go

Double A, Stud Fire (Figures 3-114 through 3-118)

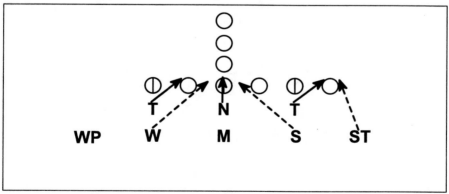

Figure 3-114. Slant strong, double A, Stud fire

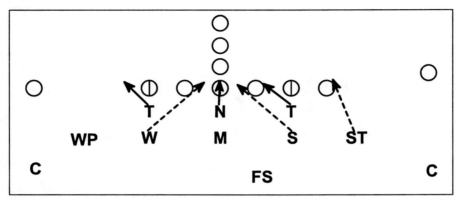

Figure 3-115. Slant weak, double A, Stud fire

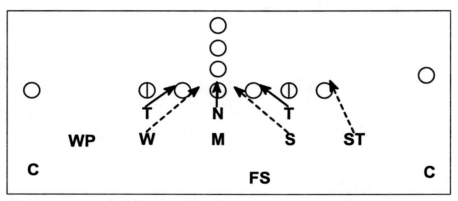

Figure 3-116. In, double A, Stud fire

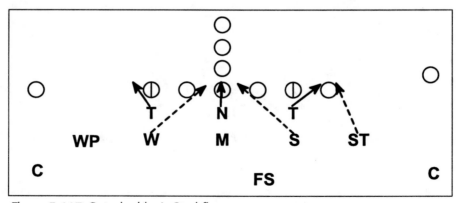

Figure 3-117. Out, double A, Stud fire

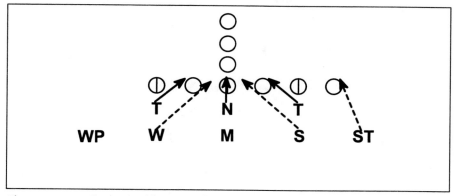

Figure 3-118. Pinch, double A, Stud fire

Double A, Whip Fire (Figures 3-119 through 3-123)

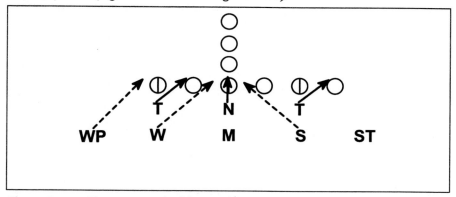

Figure 3-119. Slant strong, double A, Whip fire

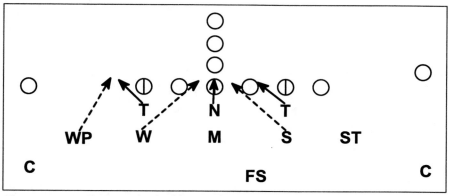

Figure 3-120. Slant weak, double A, Whip fire

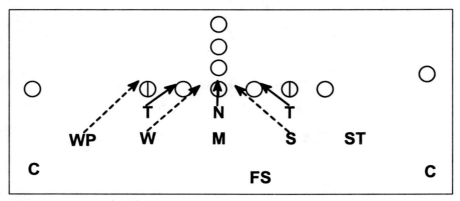

Figure 3-121. In, double A, Whip fire

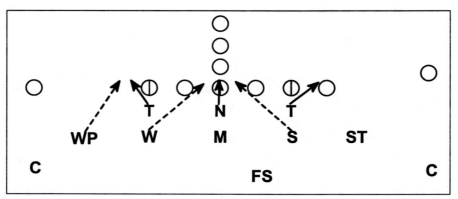

Figure 3-122. Out, double A, Whip fire

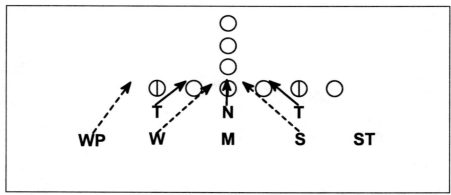

Figure 3-123. Pinch, double A, Whip fire

Seven-Man Pressures

Bat, Fire (Figures 3-124 through 3-128)

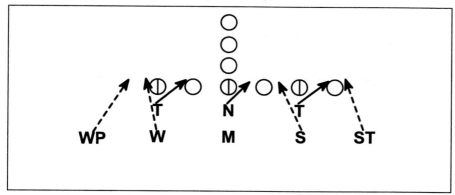

Figure 3-124. Slant strong, bat, fire

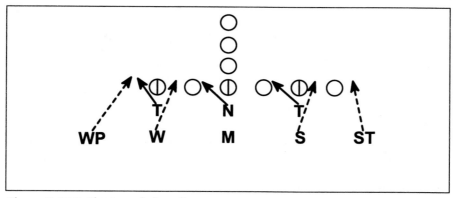

Figure 3-125. Slant weak, bat, fire

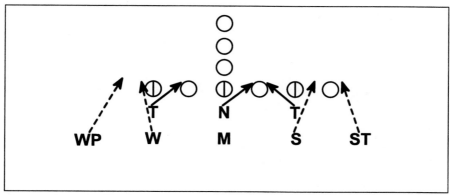

Figure 3-126. In, bat, fire

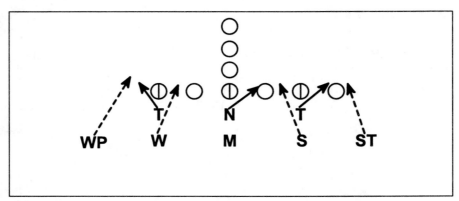

Figure 3-127. Out, bat, fire

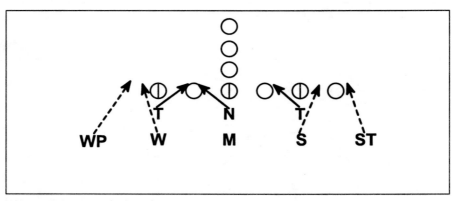

Figure 3-128. Pinch, bat, fire

Dog, Stud Fire (Figures 3-129 through 3-133)

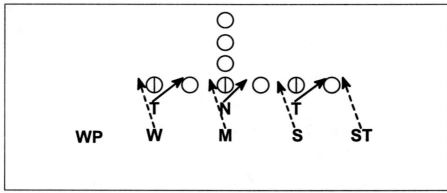

Figure 3-129. Slant strong, dog, Stud fire

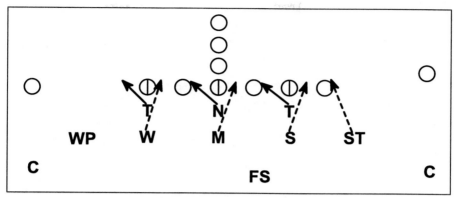

Figure 3-130. Slant weak, dog, Stud fire

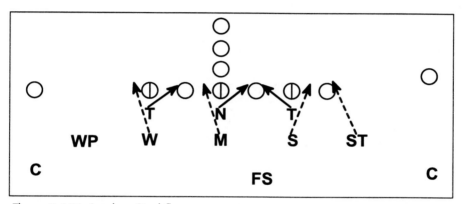

Figure 3-131. In, dog, Stud fire

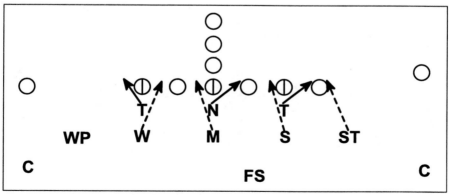

Figure 3-132. Out, dog, Stud fire

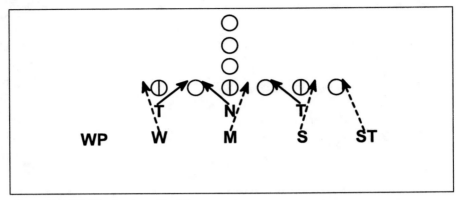

Figure 3-133. Pinch, dog, Stud fire

Dog, Whip Fire (Figures 3-134 through 3-138)

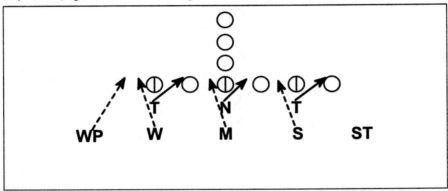

Figure 3-134. Slant strong, dog, Whip fire

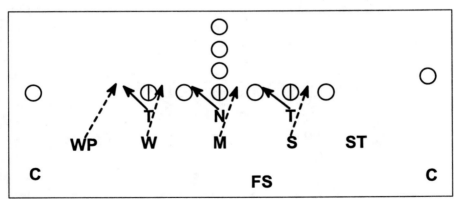

Figure 3-135. Slant weak, dog, Whip fire

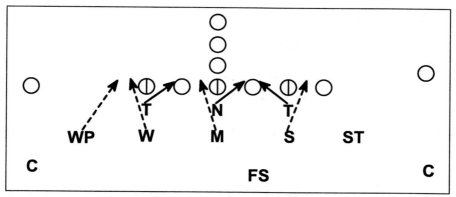

Figure 3-136. In, dog, Whip fire

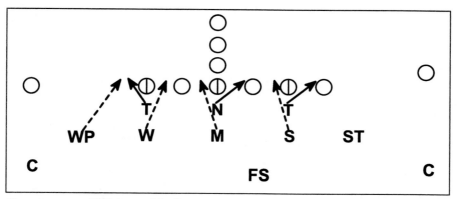

Figure 3-137. Out, dog, Whip fire

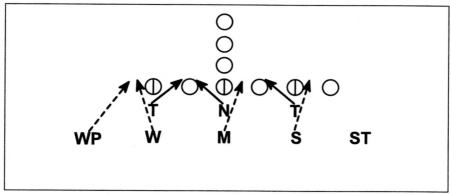

Figure 3-138. Pinch, dog, Whip fire

Eight-Man Pressures

Dog Fire (Figures 3-139 through 3-143)

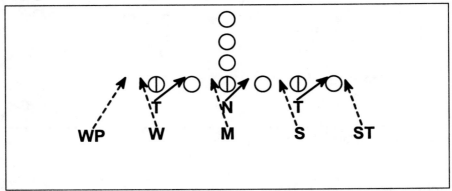

Figure 3-139. Slant strong, dog, fire

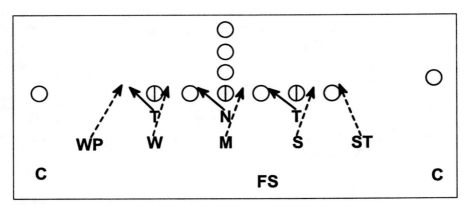

Figure 3-140. Slant weak, dog, fire

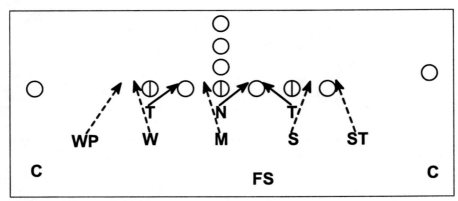

Figure 3-141. In, dog, fire

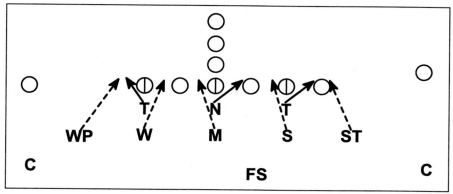

Figure 3-142. Out, dog, fire

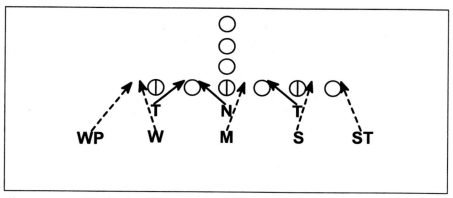

Figure 3-143. Pinch, dog, fire

Banjo

Banjo is a check used when cover 1 or man coverage is called and an outside linebacker who is assigned a man to cover is called upon to blitz. The outside linebacker can either call banjo to tell the free safety to cover his man, or he can call banjo to assign his blitz to the inside linebacker. After the strength call is made, the formation is determined, and the outside linebacker sees that he cannot blitz because of being assigned a man to cover, he will physically turn to the free safety and yell "banjo." If the free safety cannot cover the man because he is already covering someone, he will yell back "no, no" and then the outside linebacker will turn to the inside linebacker and yell "banjo." The inside linebacker will yell back "yes, yes" to tell the outside linebacker that he will perform the blitz.

4

Coverage Package

The base secondary schemes in this defense are composed of predetermined coverages that are independent of the front calls. The coverage portion of this defense is actually rather simple. By design, this defense lends itself well to any type of man coverage if you have the athletes every year to run it. On the other hand, cover 3 is better suited to this defense because of what is asked of the defensive backs regarding the running game, and because it is easier to run with lesser athletes.

Coverage Basics

- Cover 3 will be used in this defense 80 percent of the time.
- It will use some aspect of man coverage another 15 percent of the time.
- Prevent defense will be run the other 5 percent.
- The coverage package is kept simple so that the players don't have to do much thinking.
- On occasion, underneath zones will be voided when blitzes are used.
- The underneath drops will sometimes sling to cover up a blitz.
- Except in cases of cover 4 or cat cover 4, the Mike linebacker will always rush on pass plays. He will pick an empty hole and serve as secondary contain. If a time

arises when you don't want him to rush, "spy" needs to called and Mike will cover the middle zone.

- The motto of this defense is: "There may be holes, but you'd better throw it in a hurry."

Divide (Figure 4-1)

- The inside linebackers are used to divide the middle of the field.
- They will cut off any crossing routes that come across the middle of the field.

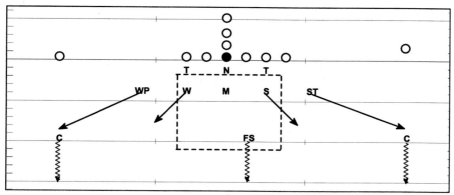

Figure 4-1. Divide the middle of the field.

Sling (Figures 4-2 and 4-3)

- Any time a roll or sprint-out action is performed by the quarterback, the underneath drop players will sling to cover any holes that may appear because of a blitz.
- The sling is to the direction of the quarterback's roll or sprint.
- In a straight dropback situation, everything stays the same.

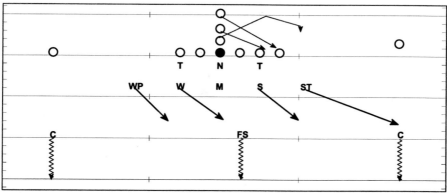

Figure 4-2. Roll right, underneath drop players slinging to the right

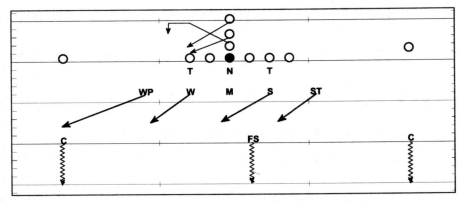

Figure 4-3. Roll left, underneath drop players slinging to the left

Coverages in the 3-5-3

Cover 3 (Figure 4-4)

- On a pass read, Mike will find an open hole and rush.
- Corners play deep outside one-thirds.
- The free safety will play deep middle one-third.
- Stud and Whip play the flats to their sides.
- Sam and Will play hook/curl to their sides.

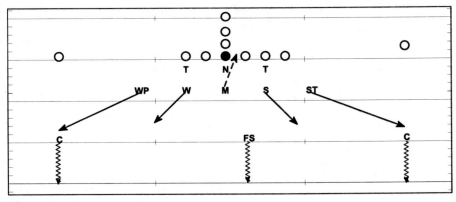

Figure 4-4. Base cover 3

Cover 3 Adjustments Versus Twins (Figure 4-5)

• Whip is head up at four to six yards.

• The weak corner and free safety are playing quarters.

• The strong corner is playing half of the field.

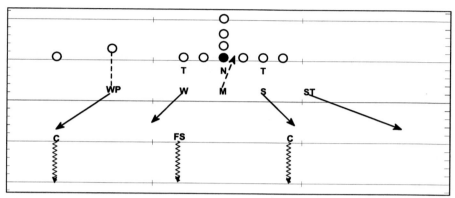

Figure 4-5. Cover 3 versus twins

Cover 3 Adjustments Versus Trips (Figure 4-6)

• Whip is on the nipple half-way between the number 3 and 4 receivers, four to six yards deep, and tries to redirect one of the two inside wide receivers.

• The weak corner and free safety are playing quarters.

• The strong corner is playing half of the field.

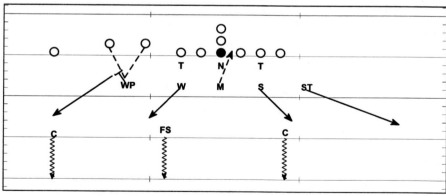

Figure 4-6. Cover 3 versus trips

Cover 3 Adjustments Versus Double Tight Ends (Figure 4-7)

- The strong corner and free safety are playing quarters.
- The weak corner is playing half of the field.
- The outside linebackers will tighten up to two-by-four off the end man on the line of scrimmage.

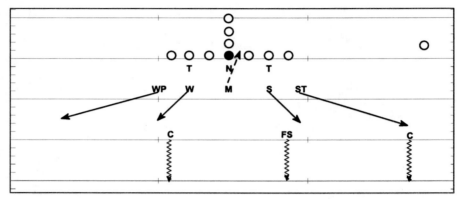

Figure 4-7. Cover 3 versus double tight ends

Cover 3 Adjustments Versus Double Tight Ends Unbalanced (Figure 4-8)

- The defensive front and linebackers will bump one full man to the unbalanced call.
- The weak corner and free safety are playing quarters.
- The strong corner is playing half of the field.
- The outside linebackers will tighten up to two-by-four off the end man on the line of scrimmage.

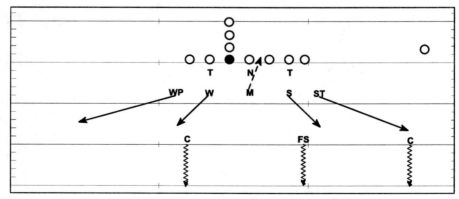

Figure 4-8. Cover 3 versus double tight ends unbalanced

- The entire front bumps one whole man toward the strength of the formation and the outside linebackers tighten up.

- Stud must be head up to outside of the wide receiver. Otherwise, the offense has angles to block everyone down.

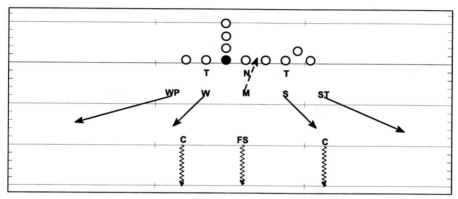

Figure 4-9. Cover 3 versus overload

Cover Man (Figure 4-10)

- Corners have number 1 to their side.
- Whip has number 2 weak.
- Free has number 2 strong or number 3 weak.
- Stud would have number 3 strong.
- On a pass read, Mike will find an open hole and rush.

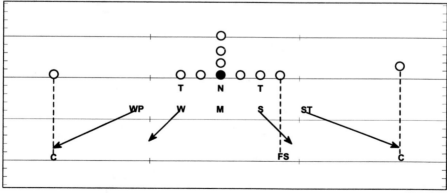

Figure 4-10. Man coverage

Cover Man Versus Twins and Trips (Figures 4-11 and 4-12)

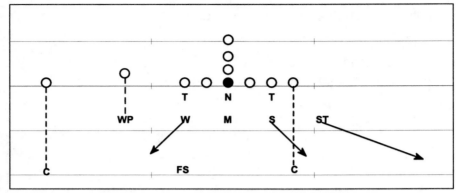

Figure 4-11. Cover man versus twins

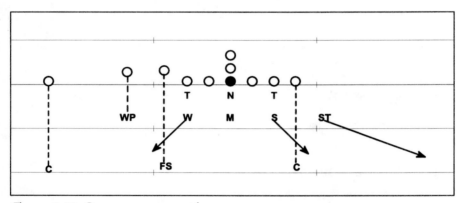

Figure 4-12. Cover man versus trips

Cover Man Adjustments/Motions (Figures 4-13 and 4-14)

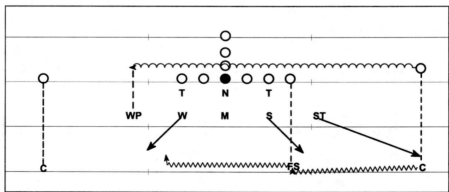

Figure 4-13. Pro to twins

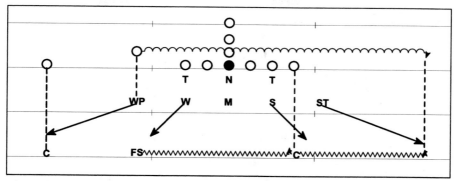

Figure 4-14. Twins to pro

Cover 1 (Man Free) (Figure 4-15)

- Corners have number 1 to their sides.
- Stud and Whip have number 2 to their sides.
- The free safety has number 3 either way.

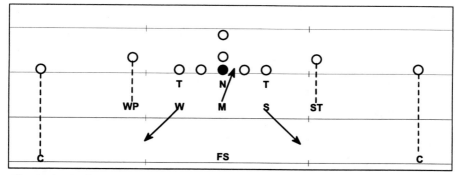

Figure 4-15. Cover 1

Cover 1 Adjustments/Motion (Figures 4-16 through 4-18)

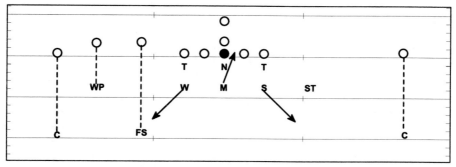

Figure 4-16. Cover 1 versus trips

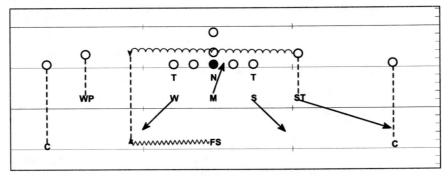

Figure 4-17. Cover 1 versus double twins motion to trips open

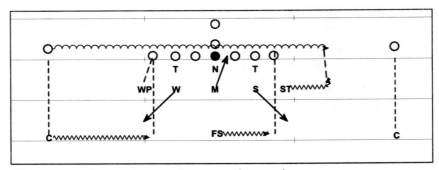

Figure 4-18. Cover 1 versus moose motion to trio

Cover 4 (Figure 4-19)

- Unless told to do so by a blitz, Mike will not rush. He will settle in the middle of the field.
- Whip will move back as a true safety.
- The Will linebacker will play weak hook/curl to the flats.

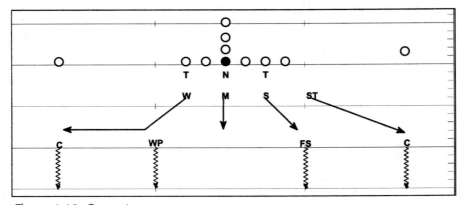

Figure 4-19. Cover 4

Cover 4 Adjustment (Figure 4-20)

• Stud will redirect one of the two inside receivers.

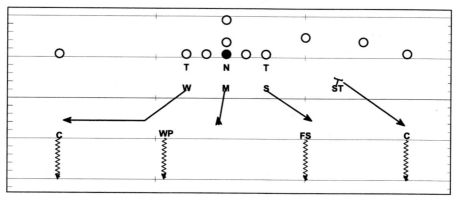

Figure 4-20. Cover 4 versus trips open

Cat Cover 4 (Figure 4-21)

• Cat will tell the Will linebacker to line up over number 2 to his side. It will be the only time that an inside linebacker will be removed from the box.

• Unless told to do so with a blitz, Mike will not rush. He will take hook/curl weak.

• Cat will only be run if a minimal run threat exists.

• Cat will usually be run versus one-back or no-back formations.

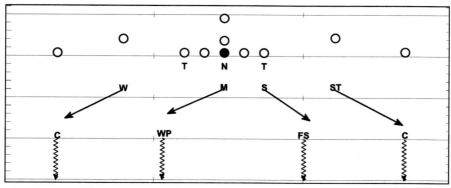

Figure 4-21. Cat cover 4

Cat Cover 4 Versus Quads (Figure 4-22)

- The coverage will condense to the quads side to help cover up that side.

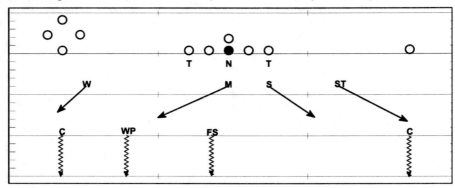

Figure 4-22. Cat cover 4 versus quads

Cat Cover 4 Versus Trips/Twins (Figure 4-23)

- Stud will redirect one of the three trips receivers.

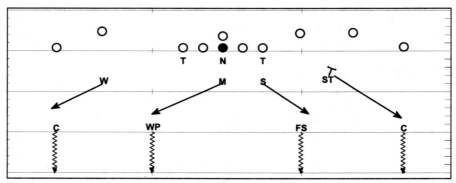

Figure 4-23. Cat cover 4 versus trips/twins

Cover 3 Sky (Figure 4-24)

- Sky tells the defense that they are going to show cover 3 and on the snap roll to cover 4 (quarters).
- The free safety will slide to the strong hash and play the deep strong middle quarter of the field.
- Whip will sprint to the weak hash and play the deep weak middle quarter of the field.
- Both corners are playing the deep outside quarters of the field.
- Mike will drop to hook/curl weak.
- The Will linebacker will cover the weak flats.

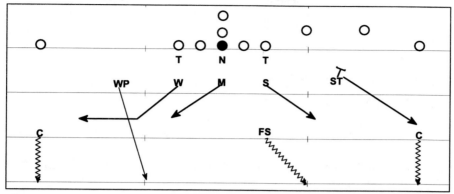

Figure 4-24. Cover 3 Sky

Defending Against the Bootleg (Figure 4-25)

What is important to remember about playing the bootleg is that pressure, not coverage, will stop this play. As soon as the outside linebacker sees split flow and the quarterback settling into his mesh, he will go to put pressure in the quarterback's face. The Will linebacker will fly across the field to help cover the weak flats. The other linebackers will sling in the direction of the quarterback's roll.

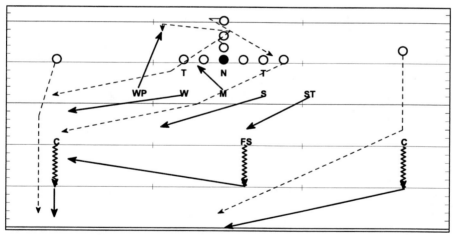

Figure Figure 4-25. Defending against the bootleg

Coverage Facts

- You can take away the quick slant through alignment.
- Everyone will try the tight end pop pass.
- Teams will try and bootleg you to death.
- Teams will rely on play action, because the nature of the 3-5-3 defense is very aggressive.
- You can rush four and be successful, because your opponent will not know where the pressure is coming from.

5

Defensive Line Play

One common question about the 3-5-3 defense is, "Is there a difference in coaching defensive linemen in the 3-5-3 versus other systems?" The answer is actually yes and no.

No—As all defensive coaches know, tackling, running, and being tough must be a part of any good defense. Remember, the defensive linemen in this defense will always slant one way or another, so they are not required to be as big and strong as in other systems. But times will arise when the defensive linemen will have to resort to more traditional techniques to accomplish what they need to do.

Yes—Because the defensive linemen in this system never take on an offensive lineman head up, they need to be taught "reading on the run." Reading on the run is a technique in which the defensive linemen will attack half a man with either a rip or by attacking the inside chest plate and then reading the block that is presented to him by the offensive linemen. After that technique is learned, the most important skills to work on are fighting pressure with pressure and not getting washed up field.

Essentials of Defensive Line Play in the 3-5-3

The 3-5-3 defense features several essentials that must be stressed every day for your defensive linemen to be productive playmakers. These essentials are as follows:

- *Get-off*—The defensive linemen must explode off the ball and cross the face of the man they are lined up across.

- *Pursuit*—Defensive coaches must stress running to the ball on every play during practice.

- *Tackling*—Players must work some aspect of tackling every day.

- *Production*—Defensive coaches need to teach their defensive linemen to be more productive in the areas of tackling, pressure, and pursuit.

- *Specificity*—Defensive coaches need to run drills that are specific to the 3-5-3. If a drill does not relate to the overall defensive scheme of the 3-5-3, don't do it.

- *Realism*—You will need to put your defensive linemen in real-life, game-type situations every day in practice.

Qualities to Look for in Defensive Linemen

The ability to run is one of the most important attributes a defensive lineman can have to be successful in this system. Defensive linemen in the 3-5-3 defense are not sled pushers. They are never asked to move offensive linemen around the field. Instead, they are asked to beat the offensive linemen with speed—to rip by them and run flat down the line of scrimmage and make tackles. To be successful in this defense, you must find players who are quick off the ball and yet strong enough to fight pressure. The defensive line consists of two tackles that typically line head up to the offensive tackles. The noseguard will line up head up to the center and he needs to be the best defensive lineman on the field. He must command a double-team from the offensive center and guards.

Defensive Line Fundamentals in the 3-5-3

Defensive line fundamentals in the 3-5-3 are broken down into eight parts. These parts need to be worked on every day in practice and be the focus of the defensive line coach's practice plans.

Alignment

Alignment needs to be worked every day. A player lining up in the correct place is a small matter that tends to be overlooked because of a coach focusing on the overall scheme.

- The defensive linemen will line up three different ways in this system:

    ✓ In base, they will be head up.

✓ In jet, they will be in a wide 5 and a wide 9.

✓ In goal line, they will be in 4 techniques.

- The defensive linemen are crowded as close to the ball as possible.

Stance

Stance is another small matter that tends to get overlooked. Getting into a correct stance is important so that the defensive lineman can explode off the ball and get to where he is assigned to go. If he is not in the correct stance, false steps and timing problems will occur.

- The proper stance is a three-point stance with the feet as close to parallel as possible.
- Linemen should keep the weight on the balls of the feet, the knees in, and the heels off the ground.
- They should turn the head and look down the line of scrimmage at the football.
- The front arm should be well in front of the head. The free arm is cocked by the face mask, ready to strike.
- The butt must be higher than the head.
- Sixty percent of the weight is on the fingertips. Linemen are "coiled springs" ready to explode.
- The feet should be no wider than shoulder-width apart.
- The defensive linemen need to be able to step with either foot.

Slant/Steps

- If the linemen are slanting to the right, they will step with the right foot. If they are slanting to the left, they will step with the left foot.
- The initial movement must be sideways and slightly up at a 45-degree angle.
- Like a sprinter coming out of the blocks, linemen must create force.
- The back must be flat.
- The numbers of the jersey should be over the knee.
- Linemen must bull the neck.
- Linemen must aim for the hip of the man they are slanting to.
- The second step must reach the outside foot of the man they are slanting across.
- They should follow quickly with the third and fourth steps
- Linemen must stay low and maintain lift leverage.
- They should get to one yard deep.

Engagement/Blow Delivery

- Defensive linemen must punch their off hand across the man they are slanting across.
- They are aiming for the hip of the man they are slanting to.
- When they make contact with the offensive lineman, they either finish their rip or, if they get stoned, bring both hands up into half of the offensive lineman's chest plate, lift, control the gap, and find the ball.
- They never want to get more than one yard up the field.
- If they ever come off unblocked, they will need to turn their shoulders and run to the inside (a trap or kick-out is coming).

Read/Pressure

- Defensive linemen will read on the run. If an offensive lineman pressures them, they need to pressure back by either crossing his face or going backdoor.
- They cannot get washed up the field. They can prevent this outcome by fighting pressure with pressure and not getting more than one yard up the field.
- If a defensive lineman slants and his man tries to cut him off, he will need to flatten down the line of scrimmage and pursue to the ball.
- Linemen can defeat the double-team block by either splitting the block or by stopping and creating a pile. The defensive lineman must not lose ground on a double-team.

Pursuit

- Defensive linemen must find the ball and take good angles to intercept the ballcarrier.
- This defensive scheme demands 11 hats to the ball on every play. Defensive coaches will not get good pursuit unless they stress running to the ball on every play in practice.
- You may want to consider additional running after practice for "loafs" when you are not getting 11 people to the ball on every play.
- Pursuit drills need not be done alone; defensive coaches can incorporate them into inside, skelly, or team practice sessions.

Tackling

All great defensive football teams pride themselves on not missing tackles. To accomplish this objective, coaches must work some aspect of tackling every day in practice. Every tackle involves six elements, all of which need to be worked into every tackling drill that is performed:

- *Feet*—Tacklers must never gather the feet and should always run through the target.
- *Eyes*—Eyes always need to be looking at the ballcarrier's numbers. The ballcarrier can juke with his head or his hips, but never with his numbers.
- *Head placement*—Keep the head out of tackling. It always goes up and across the ball.
- *Chest*—Tacklers must always lead with the chest, not with the head.
- *High cloth*—They should throw their arms up and around the ballcarrier and grab high cloth.
- *Hip roll*—To make a proper tackle, the tackler must act like he has a quarter in his cheeks and does not want it to fall out.

Pass Rush

Defensive linemen must accomplish to the following tasks involved in the pass rush:

- Each defensive lineman must get off the ball.
- He must never attack a full man.
- If he is beat to the intersection, he must flip his hips and grab cloth.
- He must always have a counter move ready.
- He only has three seconds to get to the quarterback, so he can't have any wasted movement.
- He must force the quarterback to make bad decisions.
- He must constrict the quarterback's area.
- He must not give the quarterback time to look around or throw to a secondary receiver.
- He must force the quarterback out of his area and make him throw on the run.
- He must cause the quarterback to lose confidence in his blockers.
- He must keep his feet moving upfield; if his feet stop, he has been beaten.
- He must not get out of his lane.

Since the 3-5-3 is a slanting defense, the defensive linemen will always be in "pass rush" mode. Their run reads and pass reads are no different. They slant, find the ball, and then run. Each defensive lineman must beat the offensive lineman to the intersection, which is the point at which the offensive lineman tries to cut off the defensive lineman's slant (Figure 5-1). If the defensive lineman beats the offensive lineman to the intersection, he will continue with his rip and work up the field. If the offensive lineman kicks out or back and beats the defensive lineman to the intersection, he must then flip his hips and work a traditional pass-rush move.

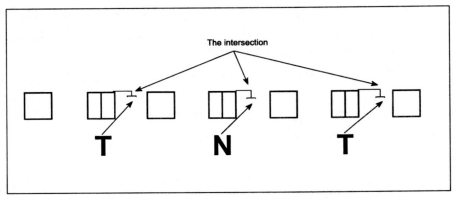

Figure 5-1. The intersection

Pass-Rush Skills

Hip Flip

- The hip flip is the most essential element of the pass rush.
- The defensive lineman must create separation with the offensive lineman or he will get held.
- By flipping his hips, the defensive lineman not only creates separation, but assures himself that the offensive lineman will only get half of his body.

Grab

- Defensive linemen must grab cloth.
- They must then propel their hips upfield.
- Finally, they must work a seamless transition from "hands in chest" to "hands on shoulder."

Bull Rush

- Everything starts from a bull rush.
- If the offensive lineman is leaning back, the defensive lineman should accelerate the feet and push back.
- The bull rush is the only move that does not involve a hip flip.
- The defensive lineman should try to push the offensive lineman into the quarterback.

- The defensive lineman should always be ready with a counter in case the offensive lineman anchors.

Swim

- The defensive lineman should pull down and in.
- Then, he should punch his arm over and get his hips upfield.
- Finally, he should slap the offensive lineman on the butt to clear his body.

Rip

- The defensive lineman must see the target—physically look at the target and aim for the biceps.
- Then, he must grab outside cloth, shoot the arm through, lift, and push up.
- Finally, he should lean into the rip and accelerate upfield.

Club

- The defensive lineman must stab off the numbers and use a head fake to that side.
- He must then club the offensive lineman with the opposite hand.
- Finally, he should rip or swim over.

Speed Rush

- The defensive lineman must quickly get off the ball.
- He must beat the blocker to the intersection (one yard wide by one yard deep).
- Finally, he must accelerate by the blocker.

Spin

- The spin move is used only when the defensive lineman is parallel with the quarterback.
- The defensive lineman reaches with the inside hand and pulls.
- He then sits down, hooks with outside hand, and swings the head around.
- Finally, he stabs the offensive lineman in the back to clear his body.

Counters

- If using the swim move, the defensive lineman should counter with the rip.
- If using the rip move, the defensive lineman should counter with the swim.

Defensive Line Practice Progression

Tennis Ball Drills

- The player lines up in his stance 10 yards in front of a coach.
- The coach drops a tennis ball from about shoulder height onto a hard surface.
- On the ball drop, the player explodes out of his stance and attempts to catch the tennis ball.
- The player must catch the ball before it bounces twice.
- This drill teaches get-off and staying low.

Get-off Drill

- The players form lines across from a blocking dummy, which is laying flat on the ground.
- The players face the blocking dummy and get in a stance.
- The coach gives a direction (right or left), which tells the defensive linemen which way they are slanting.
- The coach snaps a football and the players must explode out of their stance, rip by the bag, and stay low.
- The players sprint to the end of the dummies.
- The coach needs to be sure to yell a cadence and snap the ball at different times.
- This drill teaches players the importance of watching the football, taking proper steps, and performing a proper rip and get-off.

Flow Drill (Figure 5-2)

- This drill is the same as the get-off drill, except that after the players have ripped by the dummy, the coach will point right or left.
- The players plant, turn, and pursue in that direction.
- This drill teaches players how to change directions and get one yard deep.

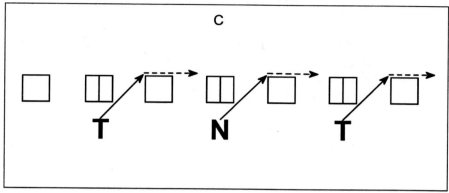

Figure 5-2. Flow drill

Get Some Drill (Figure 5-3)

- The defensive lineman runs two hoops set up as a figure eight.
- Around the first hoop, he rips with his inside arm, against other players punching at him.
- Around the second hoop, he rips with his other arm against other players punching him.
- He finishes the drill by strip tackling a dummy.
- This drill works proper body lean, arm rip, and foot movement.

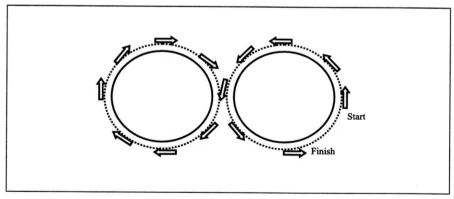

Figure 5-3. Get some drill

Backdoor Drill (Figure 5-4)

- The purpose of this drill is to recreate a situation in which a defensive lineman is following a trapping offensive lineman or has ripped into a gap and feels pressure from a down block.
- The offensive lineman will fit on the defensive lineman's hip.
- The defensive lineman will then grab the hip of the offensive lineman and go backdoor, pursuing flat down the line of scrimmage.

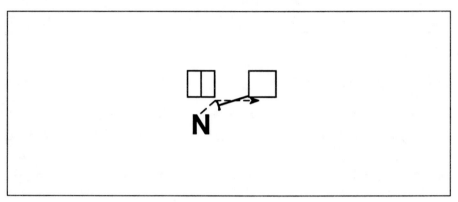

Figure 5-4. Backdoor drill

Rabbit Drill (Figure 5-5)

- Two players line up on a hoop. One player gets a three-yard head start.
- The two players run a figure eight. If player 2 catches player 1, the drill is over.
- This drill focuses on effort, pursuit, and body lean.

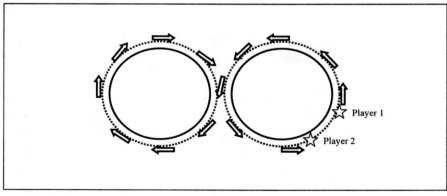

Figure 5-5. Rabbit drill

Angle Tackling Drill (Figure 5-6)

- The angle tacking drill should be the main tackling drill that the defensive linemen perform.
- A defensive lineman lines up in a stance across from another lineman and on command rips by the other player.
- The running back runs either right or left next to the offensive lineman.
- If the running back comes to the same side that the defensive lineman slanted to, the defensive lineman performs a proper angle tackle.
- If the running back runs to the opposite side of where the defensive lineman slanted, then he must plant, flow back to the running back, and make the tackle.
- This drills focuses on taking proper angles, tackling, and pursuit.

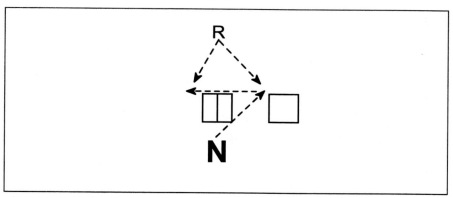

Figure 5-6. Angle tackling drill

Speed to Burn (Figure 5-7)

- Two defensive ends set up in a jet-speed rush coming off each corner.
- The defensive ends have to speed rip by an offensive lineman and strip tackle a dummy.
- Whoever gets to the dummy the fastest is the winner.
- This drill focuses on speed rush, tackling, and effort.

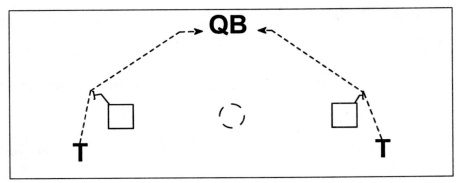

Figure 5-7. Speed to burn drill

Pass-Rush Drills

Hip Flip Drill

- Two players begin facing each other.
- The hands of the defensive lineman start on the chest of the offensive lineman.
- The defensive lineman should reach for the shoulder pad and flip hips.
- He must try to get perpendicular.
- After the hip flip drill is complete, this drill is run using all pass-rush moves—rip, swim, club, etc.

Hoops Drills

- The figure eight drill is done with two hoops together, focusing on lean and change of direction (Figure 5-8).
- The speed drill is performed with one hoop and at full speed all the way around (Figure 5-9).
- Hoops drills develop body lean and footwork.

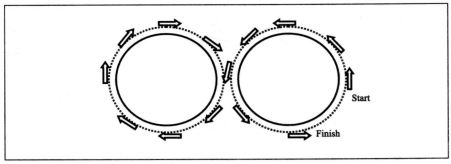

Figure 5-8. Figure eight hoops drill

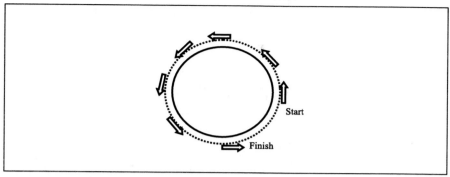

Figure 5-9. Speed hoops drill

Defensive Line Run Read Drills—One-on-One Blocks

Base Block Drill

In this drill, the nose is getting a base block from the center (Figure 5-10). Due to the slant of the nose, the base block should turn into a fan-type block, with the center trying to wash the nose up the field. The nose will slant and get to one yard deep. If the center tries to wash him up the field, the nose will either go backdoor or cross the face of the center.

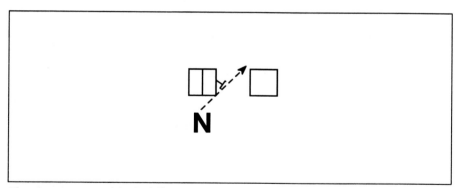

Figure 5-10. Base block drill

Reach Block Drill

This drill is an example of the weak tackle getting reached by the offensive tackle (Figure 5-11). Any time the defensive tackle feels an offensive lineman try and cut him off or reach him, the defensive lineman needs to flatten down the line of scrimmage and not allow the offensive lineman to reach his outside shoulder.

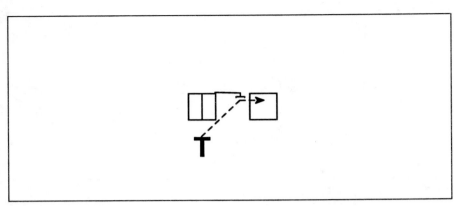

Figure 5-11. Reach block drill

Down Block Drill

This drill is an example of the strong offensive tackle down blocking in front of the strong defensive tackle (Figure 5-12). The tight end blocks down on the defensive tackle. The defensive tackle should feel pressure down from the tight end and he should go backdoor or cross the face of the tight end.

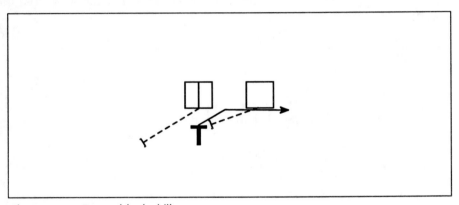

Figure 5-12. Down block drill

Pull Block Drill

This drill is an example of a tackle pull for a counter-type play (Figure 5-13). Since the defensive tackle has slanted and come off unblocked, he must turn inside and run to the center.

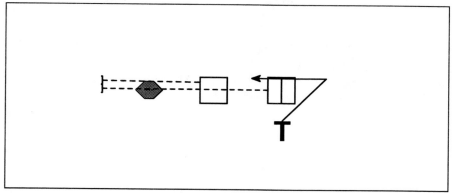

Figure 5-13. Pull block drill

Defensive Line Run Read Drills—Two-on-One Blocks

Double-Team Drill

This drill presents a double-team block between the center and strong guard (Figure 5-14). The nose has slanted strong and has met pressure from the strong guard. The nose should split the double-team if he can. If he cannot split the double team, he needs to stop and create a pile where he is. The nose must not lose ground on the double-team.

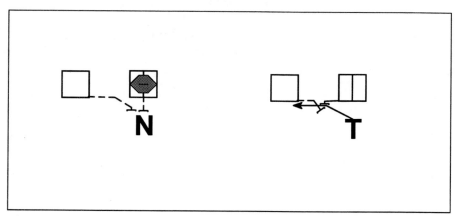

Figure 5-14. Double-team drill

Zone Chip Drill

This drill presents an example of a zone chip block between the offensive tackle and the tight end (Figure 5-15). The defensive tackle has slanted strong and the offensive tackle attempts to reach him with help from a chip by the tight end. The defensive tackle needs to first deny the reach block by the tackle and then fight the pressure from the tight end.

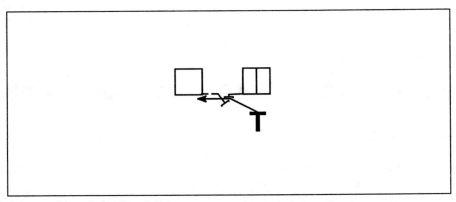

Figure 5-15. Zone chip drill

Schedule

When the defense is in its individual period (20 minutes), the defensive linemen will mostly work run reads. When the defense goes to skelly (20 minutes), the defensive linemen will shift to pass-rush fundamentals.

6

Inside Linebacker Play

The inside linebackers in the 3-5-3 system (Sam, Will, and Mike) are asked to do several things. First, in passing situations they must protect and divide the middle of the field. Second, in running situations they must fit where they belong and either make the tackle or bounce the ball to the outside. Third, the inside linebackers must cover up and defend all draws and screens that may be run by the offense.

Inside Linebacker Essentials

Inside linebackers in the 3-5-3 defense should adhere to the following rules:

- Never run sideways; always run downhill.
- Never take on an offensive player head up; always take a side and use a forearm rip.
- Never backpedal; always turn and run when doing pass drops. Avoiding backpedaling allows them to get to their drops faster.

Inside Linebacker Qualities

Inside linebackers in the 3-5-3 defense must have the following qualities:

- Speed, which is more important than size
- Good instincts
- Vision
- Good feet
- Leadership

Alignment

Alignment of the inside linebackers in the 3-5-3 defense must adhere to the following rules:

- The inside linebackers will align according to the defense called.
- The depth is three-and-a-half to four yards deep.
- The inside linebackers have total freedom of movement anywhere in their areas of play, as long as they get back to their proper alignment before the ball snaps.

Stance

An inside linebacker's stance should look as follows:

- The feet are shoulder-width apart.
- The feet are parallel.
- The knees and toes are in.
- The weight should be on the inside of the feet.
- The knees should be bent, chest out, and back flat.
- Arms should be hanging at the sides in a "clean position."

Steps

Inside linebackers must always adhere to the following rules:

- Always take a read step with the inside foot.
- The read step is simple. Pick the foot up and put it back down.
- The second step is determined by the read key.

Inside Linebacker Reads

Because the defensive front always slants, the inside linebacker reads can change from play to play depending on the slant of the defensive linemen. That said, a base set of "read rules" is used.

The inside linebackers read the man they are lined up over to the near back. The lineman gives the linebacker direction; the running back gives him the angle he needs to properly fit where he needs to. Pulling guards will take over any read.

Open Window/Closed Window

An open window is a gap in the line of scrimmage where a defensive lineman is not present. Linebackers never pass up an open window. If a gap exists, the linebacker must fill it. If a defensive lineman is in the gap, then that is a closed window and the linebacker will take the gap opposite of the lineman. Figure 6-1 illustrates how the defensive lineman is assigned the B gap and the linebacker is assigned the C gap, but because of the block of the offensive tackle and because the defensive tackle has been cut off and has to take the opposite gap, the linebacker now takes the B gap. This scenario is called a gap exchange. An important aspect of this defense is to remember that just because the linebacker is assigned a specific gap, he may have to refit somewhere else because of flow and gap exchanges. This system of linebacker reading assures that the defense will be sound against any type of false keys by the offensive line.

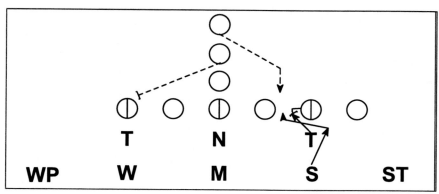

Figure 6-1. Gap exchange

Double-Team Rules

All three inside linebackers need to be drilled repeatedly on double-team rules. For example, in a double-team scenario the Mike will read the block of the center and then the flow of the back. Upon seeing a double-team by the guard, the Mike will either scrape outside the guard if the guard is on a tight track (Figure 6-2) or scrape under the down block of the guard if he is on a wide track (Figure 6-3). The Sam and Will will also carry out this same double-team play when they have a tight end to their side (Figure 6-4).

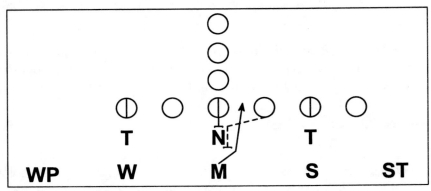

Figure 6-2. Double-team, tight track

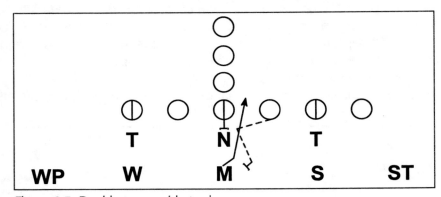

Figure 6-3. Double-team, wide track

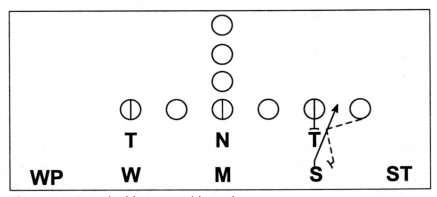

Figure 6-4. Sam double-team, wide track

Reads—Mike (Figures 6-5 through 6-8)

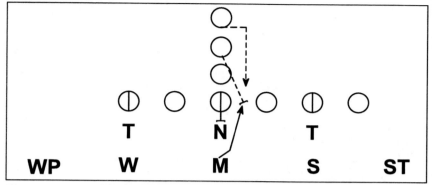

Figure 6-5. Base block, flow tight

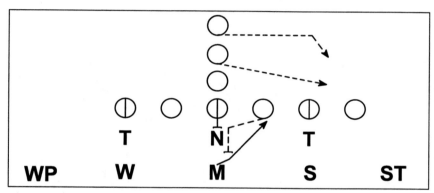

Figure 6-6. Double-team, flow strong

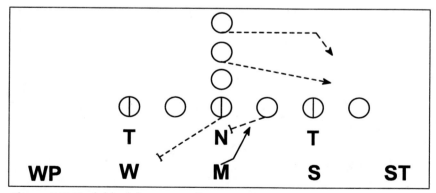

Figure 6-7. Back block by center, flow strong

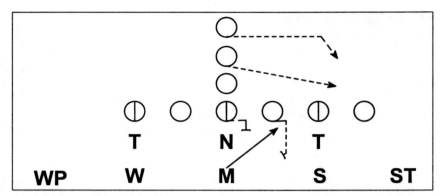

Figure 6-8. Reach block, flow wide

Reads—Sam and Will (Figures 6-9 through 6-15)

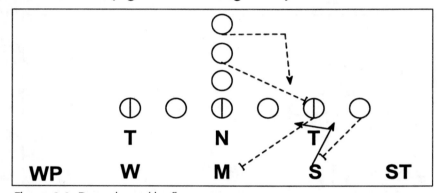

Figure 6-9. Down by tackle, flow to

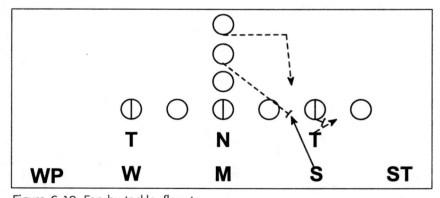

Figure 6-10. Fan by tackle, flow to

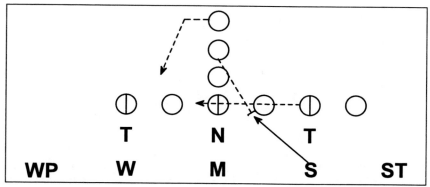

Figure 6-11. Pull away by tackle, flow to

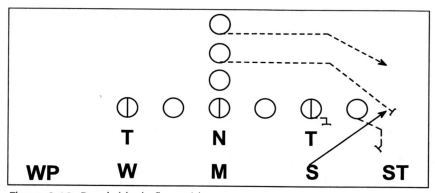

Figure 6-12. Reach block, flow wide

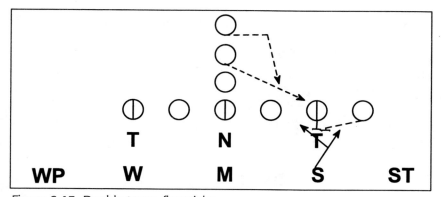

Figure 6-13. Double-team, flow tight

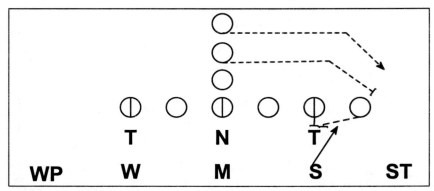

Figure 6-14. Double-team, flow wide

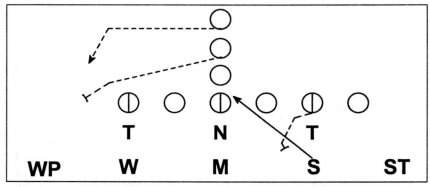

Figure 6-15. Scoop block, flow away

Blow-Delivery Rules

Inside linebackers in the 3-5-3 must adhere to the following blow-delivery rules:

- Never take on an offensive player with the whole body.
- Always use a forearm rip technique.
- Rip and remove potential blockers.
- Rip by blockers and beat them with speed.
- Concentrate on keeping the inside arm free most of the time.

Pass Drops

As soon as the linebacker recognizes a pass read, he should throw his outside elbow around his body to turn his hips to the outside. The linebacker glances to the outside to see if any receivers are crossing or dragging the field. If so, the inside linebacker attacks the crosser and tries to deviate the path of the receiver and keep him out of the middle of the field. If no receiver is crossing or dragging, the linebacker turns his head back to the quarterback while running backward to his drop zone. Once the linebacker reaches his zone (10 to 12 yards deep), he should settle in his zone and watch the quarterback for a possible sling key. Refer to chapter 4 for a detailed look at the drops and slings and dividing for the inside linebackers.

Inside Linebacker Practice Progression

Pulls Drill

- Linebackers form several lines and stretch their groins in both directions three times.
- This action will ensure that the linebackers (who are especially prone to pulled groin muscles) properly stretch their groin muscles.

Stance and Steps Drill

- Linebackers line up in several lines and show a proper stance on command.
- On the first whistle, they will perform a read step with the right foot. On the second whistle, they will step off with the right foot and run through five yards.
- They should repeat this action with both feet.
- This drill teaches athletes how to get into a proper stance and step with the correct foot. This practice will eliminate false steps and wasting time.

Cut Recover Sideways Drill (Figure 6-16)

- The players line up in one line on a spacing strip.
- On command, they run downhill with the torso straight, stomp the outside foot, and change direction down the strip.
- This drill helps prevent slipping and falling down during a change of direction.

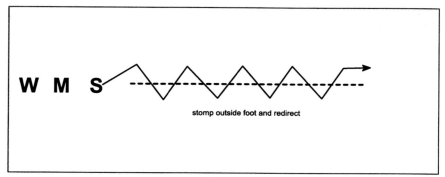

Figure 6-16. Cut recover sideways drill

Cut Recover Downhill Drill (Figure 6-17)

- The players line up in one line facing a spacing strip.
- On command, they run downhill, stomp the outside foot, and rip by a bag.
- This drill develops downhill running and blow delivery with the proper arm.

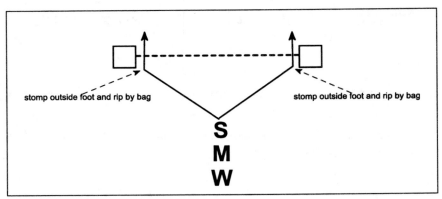

Figure 6-17. Cut recover downhill drill

Press Release Drill (Figure 6-18)

- Linebackers press the line of scrimmage. On command, they have to stop and release and get to their pass drops.
- This drill develops the ability to get back into drops after getting sucked up due to play action.

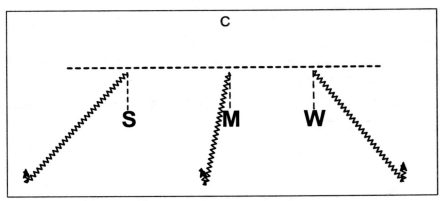

Figure 6-18. Press release drill

Angle Tackle Drill (Figure 6-19)

- The linebackers form two lines facing each other, with one acting as offense and one as defense.

- On command, the offensive man runs to a cone and the defensive player performs a perfect angle. The tackle lines rotate when done.

- The first time through the line, each linebacker will perform the tackle at half speed, only bumping the running back with the chest. This technique ensures that they are leading with the chest and not the head. The second time through the line, the linebacker performs the tackle full speed and adds arm throw, hip roll, and feet acceleration to the drill.

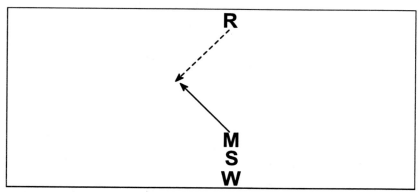

Figure 6-19. Angle tackling drill

Trap Drill

- The coach lines up an offensive line and a defensive line.

- The offensive and defensive linemen run the trap both ways and the linebackers work their reads against the trap.

- This drill gives the inside linebackers extra work against the one of the hardest plays they will have to defend.

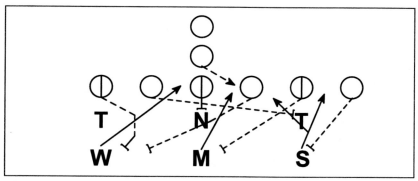

Figure 6-20. Trap drill

Pass Drops Drill (Figures 6-21 through 23)

- All three linebackers line up across the field and practice their pass drops, slings, and dividing the field.
- This drill ensures that the linebackers are performing their pass drops correctly and without any false steps.

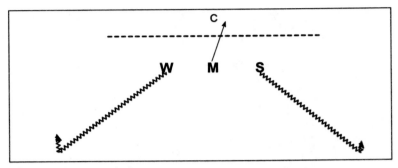

Figure 6-21. Pass drops

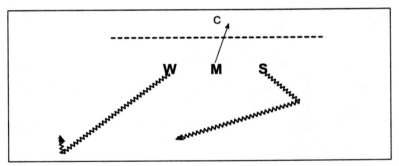

Figure 6-22. Slinging

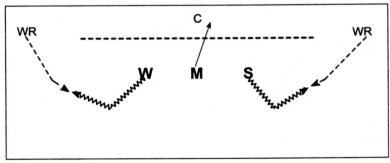

Figure 6-23. Dividing the field

Read Fill Drill (Figure 6-24)

- This drill uses a fullback leading on an inside linebacker to simulate the isolation play.
- Two bags are placed on the ground. On command, the fullback leads on an inside linebacker.
- The linebacker meets the fullback in the hole and performs a forearm rip to remove the fullback as a potential blocker.
- This drill works on filling on the isolation play against a fullback.

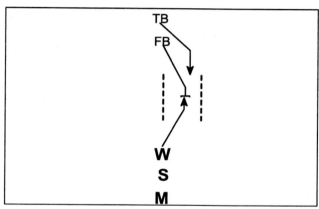

Figure 6-24. Read fill drill

Inside-Outside Drill (Figures 6-25 and 6-26)

- This drill is used to simulate an inside linebacker scraping outside on the sweep play.
- The linebacker always takes an inside-out path to the ballcarrier.
- If the tailback is inside of the fullback, the linebacker should go under the fullback.
- If the tailback is outside of the fullback, the linebacker should go over the fullback.
- This drill addresses taking the proper angle to intercept the ballcarrier.

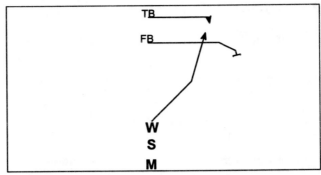
Figure 6-25. Tailback is inside of the fullback

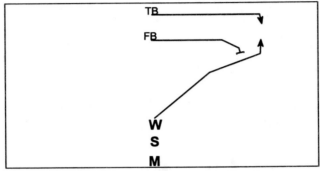
Figure 6-26. Tailback is outside of the fullback

Wave Drill (Figure 6-27)

- The linebackers begin in a stance. On command, they will all begin their pass drops in one direction.
- The coach points with either hand and the linebackers need to flip their hips and sling in the direction the coach points.

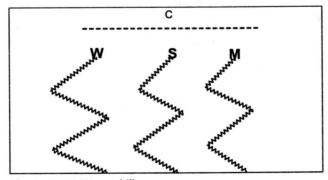
Figure 6-27. Wave drill

- This drill works on properly flipping the hips and simulates slinging across the field when the quarterback is rolling or sprinting in either direction.

Blitz Tackling Drill (Figure 6-28)

- A linebacker lines up 10 yards deep on a spacing strip.
- Other players hold bags to simulate offensive linemen.
- The linebacker sprints to a full-speed run and presses the line of scrimmage.
- The ballcarrier begins running when the linebacker begins his sprint.
- The linebacker then gears down and gains control of his body.
- The linebacker then makes a form tackle on a ballcarrier that is running downhill.

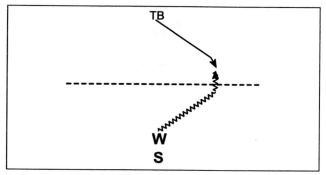

Figure 6-28. Blitz tackling drill

Open-Field Tackling Drill (Figure 6-29)

- A ballcarrier and inside linebacker line up five yards apart.
- The ballcarrier can run anywhere within a 10-yard boundary.
- The inside linebacker presses the line of scrimmage and form tackles the ballcarrier.
- This drill works the linebackers' ability to tackle in space.

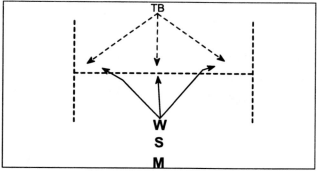

Figure 6-29. Open-field tackling drill

7

Outside Linebacker Play

Personnel

The Stud and Whip linebackers are the keys in this defense. They are hybrids that can not only defeat the block of the tight end or fullback, but also cover man-to-man if needed. If you only have one such player, you can flip sides with him.

Outside Linebacker Essentials

Outside linebackers in the 3-5-3 defensive must have the following skills:

- In coverage—Cover a receiver man-to-man if needed.
- In the run game—Take on the block of a tight end, fullback, or trapping lineman.
- Force—Act as the primary force players on every play. They must turn everything inside (always keeping the outside arm free).
- Backside—Hold and fold (as the first line of defense against a reverse or bootleg).

Alignment

Alignment of the outside linebackers in the 3-5-3 defense must adhere to the following rule:

- Freedom of movement—The base alignment is four yards wide and three-and-a-half to four yards deep off the end man on the line of scrimmage, but they have the freedom to move around and confuse the offense.

Stance

The outside linebackers' stance must look as follows:

- The feet are shoulder-width apart.
- The inside foot is up slightly.
- The knees and toes are in.
- The knees should be bent, chest out, and back flat.
- The arms should be hanging at the sides in a "clean position."

Steps

Outside linebackers must always adhere to the following rules:

- Always take a read step with the inside foot.
- The read step is simple. Pick the foot up and put it back down.
- The second step is determined by the read key.

Reads

Run Reads—Playside (Figures 7-1 through 7-6)

- The outside linebacker will read the end man on the line of scrimmage into the quarterback/near back.
- The line read gives him direction; the back read gives him angle.

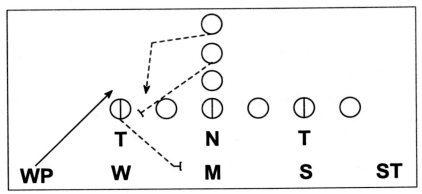

Figure 7-1. Down by tackle/tight end, flow to

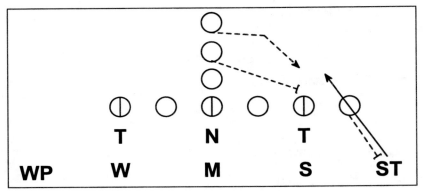

Figure 7-2. Fan by tackle/tight end, flow to

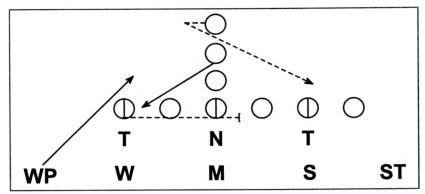

Figure 7-3. Pull away by tackle/tight end, flow to

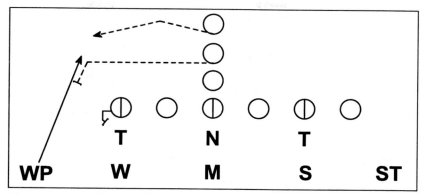

Figure 7-4. Reach by tackle/tight end block, flow wide

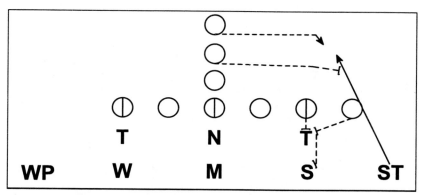

Figure 7-5. Double-team, flow wide

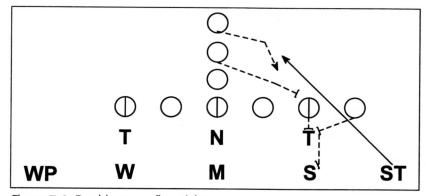

Figure 7-6. Double-team, flow tight

Run Reads—Backside (Figure 7-7)

- The outside linebacker is the first line of defense against reverses and bootlegs.
- If the outside linebacker has full flow away, he is taught to stay where he is and not move, then look for a reverse, throwback, or boot.
- When the ball has committed to the line of scrimmage, he will turn and "roll to post."

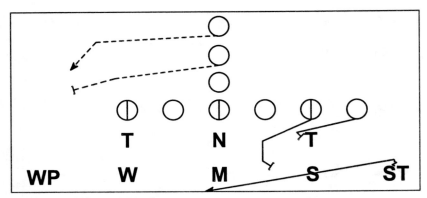

Figure 7-7. Scoop block, flow away

Pass Reads

Refer to Chapter 4 for the coverage responsibilities of the outside linebackers.

Outside Linebacker Practice Progression

The outside linebackers perform some of the same drills as the inside linebackers, in addition to the outside linebacker–specific drills described in this section. Refer to Chapter 6 for descriptions of the following drills:

- Pulls drill
- Stance and steps drill
- Cut recover sideways drill
- Cut recover downhill drill
- Press release drill
- Angle tackle drill
- Pass drops drill
- Inside-outside drill
- Wave drill

- Blitz tackling drill
- Open-field tackling drill

Press Drops Interception (Figure 7-8)

- The outside linebackers align along a spacing strip, spread out in their normal presnap alignments.
- On command, the outside linebackers press the line of scrimmage.
- On the second command, they begin their pass drops to specific spots on the field.
- After the linebackers have completed their drops (10 to 12 yards deep), they settle in their zone, reading the eyes of the quarterback.
- The quarterback throws a football somewhere in the zone of the outside linebacker.
- The outside linebacker intercepts the ball, yells "wetsu" (which stands for "we eat this stuff up"), tucks the ball away, and runs for the goal line.
- This drill develops recognition of the run/pass read, seeing the ball thrown, and interception skills.

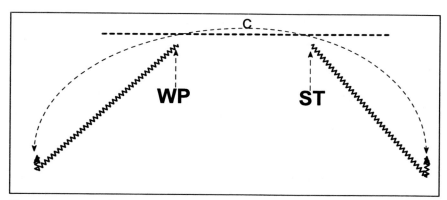

Figure 7-8. Press drops interception

Instinct Drill

- The outside linebackers align along a spacing strip, spread out in their normal presnap alignments.
- On command, the outside linebackers press the line of scrimmage.
- The coach shows the outside linebackers one of four simulated play actions.
- First, the coach shows the outside linebackers a toss sweep read (Figure 7-9).
- The outside linebacker to the playside immediately presses the line of scrimmage.
- The backside linebacker holds where he is until the ball is committed to the line of scrimmage. Then, he will roll to post.

- Next, the coach simulates a straight dropback pass (Figure 7-10).
- The outside linebackers read pass and drop to their specific drop areas.
- Next, the coach simulates a rollout pass (Figure 7-11).
- The outside linebackers practice slinging across the field.
- Finally, the coach shows the linebackers a bootleg-action play (Figure 7-12).
- The outside linebacker to the playside sees the quarterback settle in the mesh with the tailback.
- When the playside outside linebacker sees this mesh settle, he immediately pressures the quarterback in the backfield.
- The backside outside linebacker starts his sling across the field.

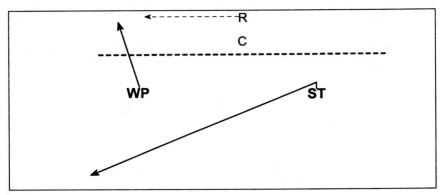

Figure 7-9. Toss sweep

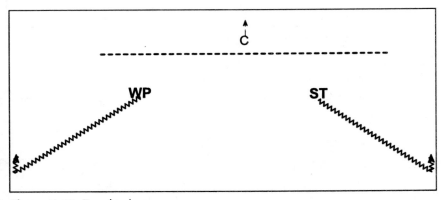

Figure 7-10. Dropback pass

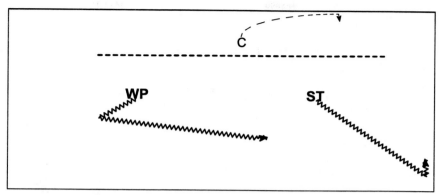

Figure 7-11. Rollout pass

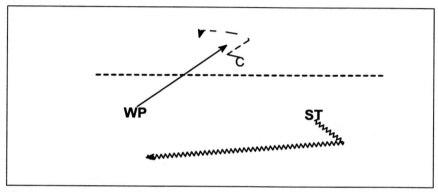

Figure 7-12. Bootleg-action play

Matador Drill (Figure 7-13)

• This drill begins with an outside linebacker facing four other players who are staggered in front of him.

• The objective of this drill is for the outside linebackers to rip through blocks to get to the ballcarrier.

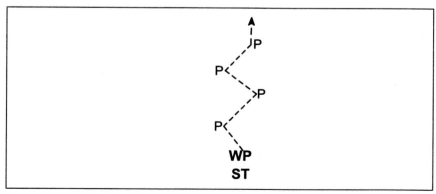

Figure 7-13. Matador drill

One-on-One Pass Rush

- The object of this drill is for the outside linebackers to practice the pass-rush skills that they will use when rushing off the edge.
- The outside linebackers practice the rip, swim, club, and speed rush moves versus an offensive lineman.

Man-Coverage Drills

The outside linebackers work man-coverage drills with the defensive backs. The primary drills that are worked on are as follows. Refer to Chapter 8 for descriptions of these drills:

- Stance and backpedal drill
- Quick turn drill
- Down the line drill
- Flip hips and run drill
- Flip hips and break on in and out routes drill
- Break on the ball drill

8

Defensive Backs Play

Due to the nature of the position, defensive backs are in the spotlight more when they do bad things than when they do well. To prevent bad things from happening, defensive backs must concentrate during every moment of the game. They must know their responsibilities for every situation and every formation in football. Defensive backs must be the best-conditioned athletes on the field, as they are required to run long distances at full speed on every down. Communication is of the utmost importance in defensive back play. They cannot be shy when calling out formations, personnel, strengths, and plays. All three defensive backs in this system must be take-charge leaders who do not shy away from their leadership roles.

Essentials of Defensive Back Play

Defensive backs in the 3-5-3 defense must adhere to the following rules:

- Eliminate the deep pass.
- Eliminate the long run.
- Come up with the big play.
- Force turnovers.
- Gain field position.

- Stop offensive momentum.
- Score on defense.

Defensive Back Terminology

Alley—The seam between the end man on the line of scrimmage and the primary force player

Arc—An outside and up-the-field maneuver by the tight end

Ball—A call that is made when the quarterback releases the football on a pass

Banjo—A check used when cover 1 or man coverage is called and an outside linebacker who is assigned a man to cover is called upon to blitz

Bootleg—The quarterback keeping the ball away from the flow of the backs

Check—A call alerting teammates to a defensive audible

Contain—Outside support forcing the ballcarrier inside

Crosser—A receiver running laterally from one side of the field to the other

Crack—A block coming from a split out receiver toward the line of scrimmage

Dropback—When the quarterback retreats from the line of scrimmage

Delay—A route of a delaying nature by a back or receiver after an area has been cleared

Flex—A three-to-five-yard split by a tight end

Kick-out—An inside/outside block coming from the line of scrimmage to remove the force player

Motion—Elongated movement by a back or receiver

Pursuit angle—An angle or line that is the quickest way to catch the ballcarrier

Reverse—When the ball starts one way and then changes direction

Roll—When the quarterback is slightly moving his pass drop right or left

Sky—Tells the defense that they are going to show cover 3 and on the snap roll to cover 4 (quarters)

Sprint—When the quarterback is quickly moving his pass drop right or left

Wetsu—A call made when the ball has been intercepted that stands for "We eat this stuff up"

Stance

The stance of a defensive back must look as follows:

- A narrow base is used, with the feet under the armpits.
- Corners will have the outside foot slightly up, with a toe-instep relationship.
- The free safety will use a stance with the feet parallel.
- The weight must be over the toes and on the inside balls of the feet.
- The knees and waist should be slightly bent, with the pads over the toes.
- The shoulders should be square to the line of scrimmage.
- The arms should be relaxed and in front of the body.
- The eyes should be turned to the inside for pass/run keys.
- The stance must be as relaxed as possible.

Backpedal

A properly executed backpedal will have the defensive backs executing the following steps:

- Explode back off the upfield foot.
- Push back from the balls of the feet through the hips.
- Pull back with the hips to create momentum.
- Stride comfortably, with weight on the balls of the feet.
- Maintain a straight line from the ground through the chest.
- Guard against the chest being too far past the balls of the feet, either forward or backward.
- Use a smooth arm action.
- Pull the body back with the elbows in a rhythmic motion.

Two-Step Recovery

The two-step recovery, which is the basis of proper defensive back play, must be drilled until all players have it mastered. Players must adhere to the following rules:

- During the backpedal, plant the back foot and then bring the front foot to the back foot.
- Step forward with the original back foot into a forward sprint.
- Always keep the upper body on the same plane and maintain a forward lean.

Drive

"Drive" means to come out of the backpedal to the ball or receiver. To properly drive, a player must do the following:

- Drive the rear elbow to the receiver or ball.
- Run to the break point.
- Avoid an elongated stride plant with the opposite foot.
- Make sure to keep the feet under the framework of the body at all times.
- The break needs to be a smooth change in momentum from backward to forward.

Quick Turn

The quick turn is used to readjust on routes after the defensive back has been forced to leave his backpedal. A quick turn involves the following actions:

- Roll with the receiver/ball by throwing the opposite elbow into him.
- Use momentum to roll the body.

Transition

"Transition" means to come out of a backpedal and run a straight line to close on deep routes. To make a proper transition, the player must do the following:

- When the defensive back's cushion is broken, his hips must open and he must accelerate.
- To open the hips smoothly, drive the elbow downfield.

Leverage

Horizontal leverage is especially important when playing good man defense. The defensive backs must adhere to the following rules:

- After establishing inside or outside leverage by alignment, maintain this leverage while in a backpedal.
- Grab inside or outside leverage with the appropriate foot.
- Do not cross inside over outside or outside over inside.
- Work to keep a one-foot horizontal leverage and a one-to-three-foot vertical leverage.

Numbers Rule

Any time a receiver lines up outside the numbers, the defensive back should not widen with him. The corners should line up on the number and backpedal toward the sideline, effectively closing the gap between himself and the receiver (Figure 8-1).

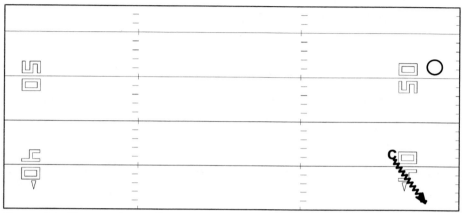

Figure 8-1. The numbers rule

Cover 3 (Base Coverage) Techniques

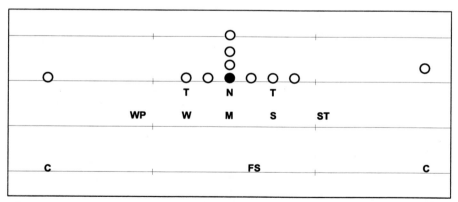

Figure 8-2. Cover 3

Corners

Alignment—They can vary their alignment anywhere from six to 10 yards off the receiver, with inside leverage.

Stance—They must keep the outside foot up.

Key—Quarterback to receiver

Responsibility—Deep outside one-third zone

Versus Run

- All run responsibilities will be late.
- If the wide receiver cracks on the outside linebacker, the corner must yell "crack" and become the primary force player (Figure 8-3).
- Against any other key, he must backpedal and maintain proper leverage.

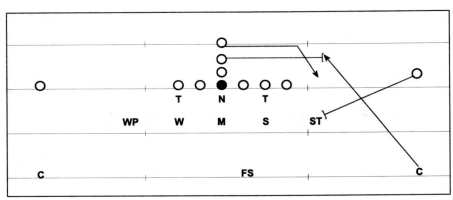

Figure 8-3. Corner replaces when Stud is cracked

Versus Pass

- The corners need to start fast in their backpedals while reading the quarterback.
- They must backpedal until the four-yard cushion is broken, and then turn the hips inside and keep proper position and leverage on the receiver.
- The corners must know what the inside receiver is doing.
- If the inside receiver crosses the corner's face, the corner must be alert for the wheel route.
- The corner will run with the post until an inside receiver crosses his face, and then he will pass the outside receiver off to the free safety and play the deep outside one-third (Figure 8-4).

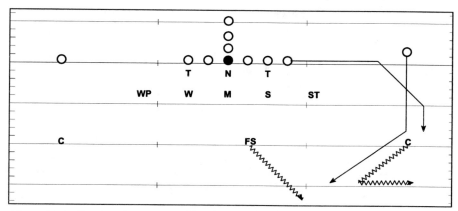

Figure 8-4. Corner play versus wheel route by tight end

Free Safety

Alignment—He can vary his alignment anywhere from six to 10 yards off the receiver, with inside leverage.

Stance—The feet should be parallel.

Key—Ball to number 2 receiver

Responsibility—Deep middle one-third zone

Versus Run

- If the ball is run strong and the tight end blocks down, the free safety will be responsible for the quarterback to pitch on option (Figure 8-5).
- If he reads sweep or lead option, the free safety will be responsible for alley to pitch (Figure 8-6).
- If the ball comes his way and the tight end is arc releasing, the free safety will be responsible for the dump pass first, then fill the alley (Figure 8-7).

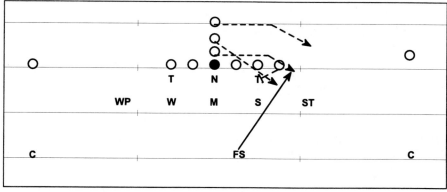

Figure 8-5. Down block by the tight end, the free safety is responsible for quarterback

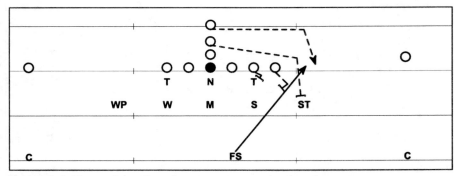

Figure 8-6. Free safety play versus a sweep or lead option

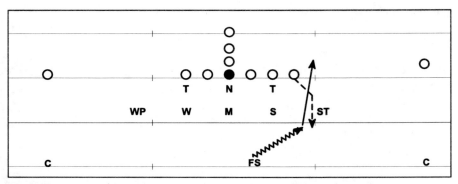

Figure 8-7. Free safety play versus an arc release by the tight end

Versus Pass

- If the free safety reads pass, he needs to check the release of number 2.
- If number 2 releases down and to the middle third, the free safety will be responsible for him (Figure 8-8).
- If number 2 goes to the flat or crosses, the free safety must look for a post pattern by a wide receiver (Figure 8-9).
- The free safety must work for depth to play the post but be ready to react to the curl pattern.

Man-Coverage Techniques

Man coverage is a basic man-to-man coverage with no help deep. The corners must play inside of their receivers to prevent the post for the touchdown. In man coverage, the defense is counting on a blitz to prevent the quarterback from having time to throw deep (Figure 8-10).

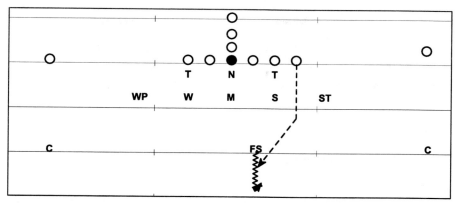

Figure 8-8. Free safety play versus number 2 down the middle of the field

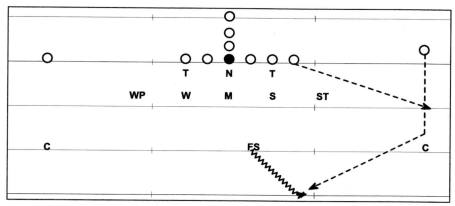

Figure 8-9. Free safety play versus number 2 flat or crossing

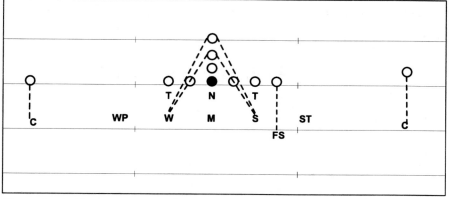

Figure 8-10. Man coverage assignments versus a pro right formation

Corners

Alignment—The corners should be four to six yards deep and one yard outside versus a split-out receiver. Versus a tight end, he should line up five to six yards deep and as head up as possible.

Stance—Outside foot up

Key—Number 1 receiver to his side

Responsibility—Man-to-man coverage anywhere on the field

Versus Run

- All run responsibilities will be late.
- If the wide receiver cracks on the outside linebacker, the corner must yell "crack" and become the primary force player.
- Versus a tight end, the corners will have the secondary force on their side.

Versus Pass—Man-to-man on the number 1 receiver

Free Safety

Alignment—He will have number 2 strong or number 3 weak. The free safety should line up five to six yards deep, shaded to the inside.

Stance—Feet parallel

Key—Ball to number 2 receivers

Responsibility—Man-to-man coverage anywhere on the field

Versus Run—Run reads are the same as in zone coverage, but a step or two slower.

Versus Pass—Man-to-man with assigned receiver

Cover 1 (Man Free) Techniques

Cover 1 (man free) is a man coverage in which both corners and both outside linebackers are assigned a man to cover. The free safety plays free over the top (Figure 8-11).

Corners

Alignment—The corners line up four to six yards deep and one yard outside versus a split-out receiver. Versus a tight end, they should line up five to six yards deep and as head up as possible.

Stance—Outside foot up

Key—Number 1 receiver to his side

Responsibility—Man-to-man coverage anywhere on the field

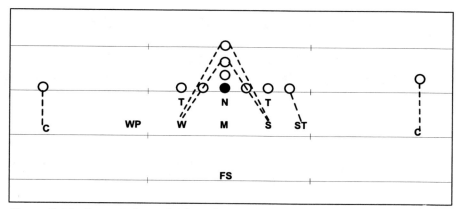

Figure 8-11. Cover 1 (man free) assignments versus a pro right formation

Versus Run

- All run responsibilities will be late.
- If the wide receiver cracks on the outside linebacker, the corner must yell "crack" and become the primary force player.
- Versus a tight end, the corners will have secondary force on their side.

Versus Pass—Man-to-man on the number 1 receiver

Free Safety

Alignment

- The free safety will have number 3 strong or weak. He should line up five to six yards deep shaded to the inside.
- If no number 3 exists either way, the free safety lines up 10 to 12 yards deep in the middle of the field.

Stance—Feet parallel

Key—Ball to both number 2 receivers

Responsibility—Deep help for underneath man-coverage players

Versus Run—Run reads are the same as in zone coverage, but a step or two slower.

Versus Pass

- The free safety plays centerfield and helps out where needed in deep zones.

- He can be used to double-cover a receiver.

Cover 4 (Quarters) Techniques

Cover 4 is used as a prevent pass coverage. The primary job of the defensive backs is the prevention of the home run ball. The defensive backs will keep backpedaling and let all crosses, rubs, and wheel routes happen underneath them (Figure 8-12).

Corners

Alignment—Corners should line up 10 to 12 yards deep and one yard inside versus a split-out receiver. Versus a tight end, they line up 10 to 12 yards deep and as head up as possible.

Stance—Outside foot up

Key—Quarterback to the number 1 receiver to that side

Responsibility—Deep outside quarter of the field

Versus Run

- All run responsibilities will be late.

- If the wide receiver cracks on the outside linebacker, the corner must yell "crack" and become the primary force player.

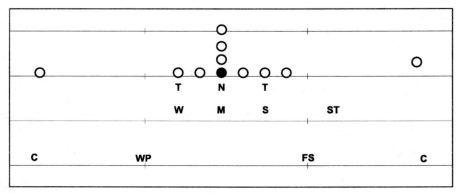

Figure 8-12. Cover 4 (quarters) alignments versus a pro right formation

Versus Pass

- Corners must start fast in their backpedals while reading the quarterback.
- They must backpedal until the four-yard cushion is broken, and then turn the hips inside, keeping proper position and leverage on the receiver.
- If the inside receiver crosses his face, the corner needs to be alert for the wheel route.
- The corner will run with the post until an inside receiver crosses his face, and then he will pass the outside receiver off to the free safety and play the deep outside one-third.
- They must keep everything in front of them and not give up the home run.
- They must not chase a receiver out of their zones.
- When in doubt, corners should keep backpedaling.

Free Safety

Alignment—The free safety should line up on the strong hash.

Stance—Feet parallel

Key—Ball to number 2 receivers

Responsibility—Strong deep middle quarter of the field

Versus Run

- If the ball is run strong and the tight end blocks down, the free safety will be responsible for quarterback to pitch on option.
- If he reads sweep or lead option, the free safety will be responsible for alley to pitch.
- If the ball comes to the free safety and the tight end is arc releasing, the free safety will be responsible for the dump pass first, then fill the alley.

Versus Pass

- If he reads pass, the free safety needs to immediately backpedal to the deep strong middle quarter of the field.
- He should work for depth to play the post and be aware of the curl underneath.
- He must keep everything in front of him and not give up the home run.
- He must not chase receivers out of his zone.
- When in doubt, he should keep backpedaling.

Cover 3 Sky Techniques

Cover 3 sky is used as a prevent pass coverage or to take away the backside skinny post. The primary job of the defensive backs is the prevention of the home run ball. The defensive backs will keep backpedaling and let all crosses, rubs, and wheel routes happen underneath them. On the snap of the ball when getting a pass read, the Whip linebacker will run back to the deep weak middle quarter of the field. The free safety will slide to the deep strong middle quarter. This coverage is designed to look like cover 3 but actually change into a prevent coverage (cover 4) (Figure 8-13).

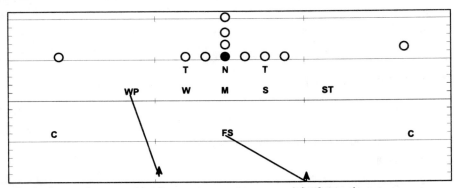

Figure 8-13. Cover 3 sky alignments versus a pro right formation

Corners

Alignment—Corners can vary their alignment anywhere from six to 10 yards off the receiver with inside leverage.

Stance—Outside foot up

Key—Quarterback to the number 1 receiver to their side

Responsibility—Deep outside quarter of the field

Versus Run

- All run responsibilities will be late.
- If the wide receiver cracks on the outside linebacker, the corner must yell "crack" and become the primary force player.

Versus Pass

- Corners must start fast in their backpedals while reading the quarterback.
- They must backpedal until the four-yard cushion is broken, and then turn the hips inside, keeping proper position and leverage on the receiver.
- If the inside receiver crosses his face, the corner must be alert for the wheel route.

- The corner will run with the post until an inside receiver crosses his face, and then he will pass the outside receiver off to the free safety and play the deep outside one-third.
- The corners must keep everything in front of them and not give up the home run.
- They must not chase receivers out of their zones.
- When in doubt, corners should keep backpedaling.

Free Safety

Alignment—The free safety should line up on the strong hash.

Stance—Feet parallel

Key—Ball to number 2 receiver

Responsibility—Middle of the field, unless dictated otherwise by a formation adjustment

Versus Run

- If the ball is run strong and the tight end blocks down, the free safety is responsible for quarterback to pitch on option.
- If he reads sweep or lead option, he will be responsible for alley to pitch.
- If the ball comes to the free safety and the tight end is arc releasing, he will be responsible for the dump pass first then fill the alley.

Versus Pass

- If he reads pass, the free safety must immediately backpedal to the deep strong middle quarter of the field.
- He should work for depth to play the post and be aware of the curl underneath.
- He must keep everything in front of him and not give up the home run.
- He must not chase receivers out of his zone.
- When in doubt, the free safety must keep backpedaling.

Defensive Backs Practice Progression

Stance and Backpedal Drill (Figure 8-14)

- The defensive backs show a proper stance and, on command, backpedal 10 yards.
- On the second command, they stop and use a two-step recovery and sprint forward 10 yards.

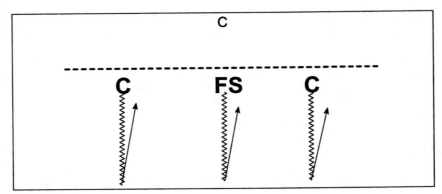

Figure 8-14. Stance and backpedal drill

Weave Drill (Figure 8-15)

• The defensive backs backpedal and, on command, flip the hips 45 degrees each way as dictated by the coach's command.

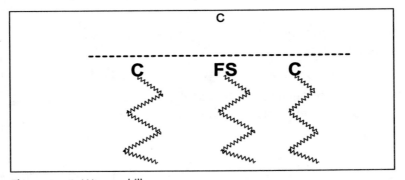

Figure 8-15. Weave drill

Drive Drill (Figure 8-16)

• On command, the defensive backs begin to backpedal and then, after 10 to 15 yards, use a two-step recovery and drive forward as if to close on a receiver who has broken off his route.

Quick Turn Drill (Figure 8-17)

• On command, a wide receiver runs a post corner and the defensive back employs a quick-turn technique to recover and close the gap.

Down the Line Drill (Figure 8-18)

• The defensive back backpedals straight back for five yards, and then uses a two-step recovery and sprints at a 45-degree angle for five yards. He should repeat this action continuously down the line.

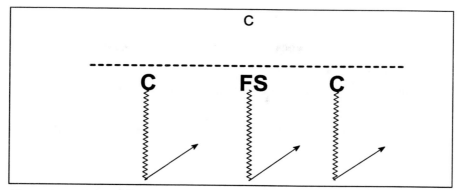

Figure 8-16. Drive drill

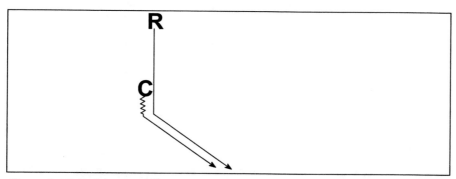

Figure 8-17. Quick turn drill

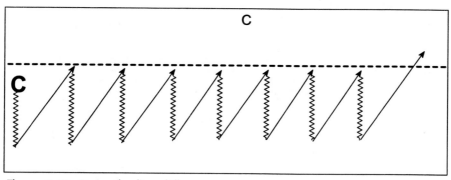

Figure 8-18. Down the line drill

Flip Hips and Run Drill (Figure 8-19)

- The defensive back backpedals for 10 yards and then simulates that his cushion has been broken and the receiver is running vertical up the field.
- He must flip the hips to the inside in zone coverage and to the receiver in man coverage.
- Once the hips are turned, he performs a full forward sprint down the line.

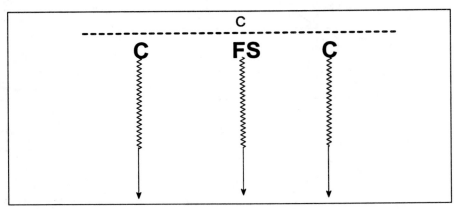

Figure 8-19. Flip hips and run drill

Flip Hips and Break on In and Out Routes Drill (Figure 8-20)

- The defensive back backpedals for 10 yards and then simulates that his cushion has been broken and the receiver is running an in or out pattern.
- He must flip the hips according to coverage and break toward the receiver.
- This drills addresses one of the hardest skills for a defensive back to perform.

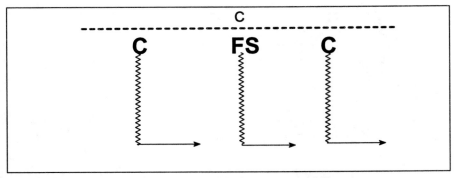

Figure 8-20. Flip hips and break on in and out routes drill

Break on the Ball Drill (Figure 8-21)

- The defensive back backpedals for 10 yards and uses a two-step recovery technique to break at a 45-degree angle.
- The coach throws a ball to be intercepted by the defensive back.
- He must catch the ball, yell "wetsu," and sprint through the line.
- Perform this drill to the right and left.

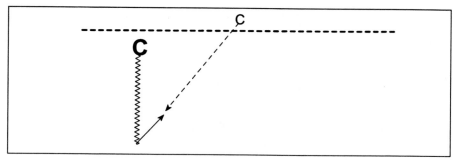

Figure 8-21. Break on the ball drill

Open-Field Tackling Drill (Figure 8-22)

- A ballcarrier and defensive back line up 5 yards apart.
- The ballcarrier can run anywhere within a 10-yard boundary.
- The defensive back backpedals, performs a two-step recovery technique, and form tackles the ballcarrier.

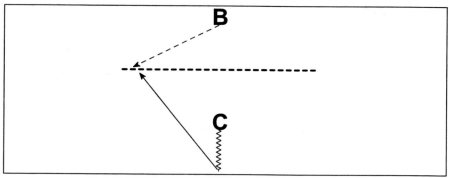

Figure 8-22. Open-field tackling drill

Angle Tackling Drill (Figure 8-23)

- A ballcarrier and defensive back line up 5 yards apart.
- The ballcarrier runs at a 45-degree angle downhill.
- The defensive back backpedals, performs a two-step recovery technique, and performs an angle tackle on the ballcarrier.

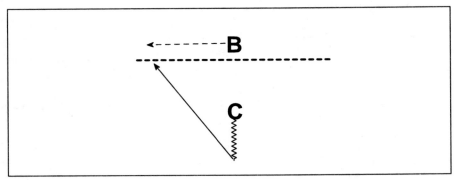

Figure 8-23. Angle tackling drill

One-on-One Situation Route Drill

- Have receivers run routes so that the defensive backs must react to different routes.
- Use all coverages.

Group Situation Route Drill

- Have more than one receiver at a time run routes so that the defensive backs must react to the routes.
- Use all coverages.

Run Support Drill

- Use all coverages versus all formations against an opponent's offensive plays.
- Teach run force, running the alley, secondary run support, and pursuit angles.

Coverage Adjustments Drill

- Check all coverages by formations and motions for needed adjustments.

9

Defending Against Power Formations, Power Runs, and the Option

The theory behind defending power formations is as follows:

- The defense must not get outflanked by the formation.
- The linebackers and defensive backs must always check for play action.
- Inside linebackers bounce everything to the outside.
- Outside linebackers force everything inside.
- Defensive backs come up late on the run.
- Defensive linemen must not give up ground on double-teams.

The 3-5-3 defense considers any type of double-tight-end formation to be a power formation. When facing such a formation, the outside linebackers must tighten up to two yards by four yards off the end man on the line of scrimmage. Examples of power formations include those presented in Figures 9-1 through 9-5.

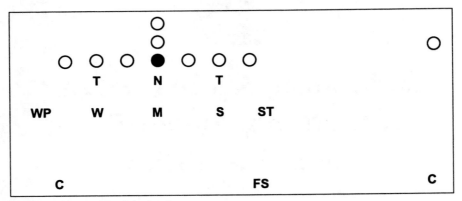

Figure 9-1. Double tight end

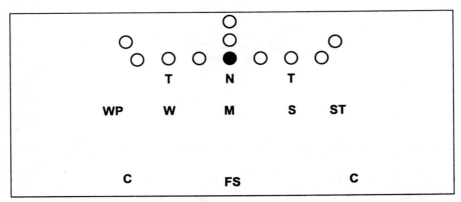

Figure 9-2. Double tight end double wing

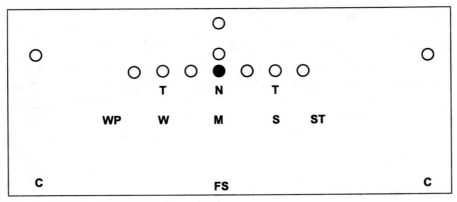

Figure 9-3. Double tight end one back

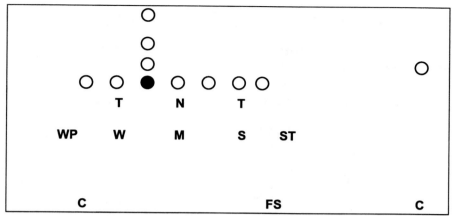

Figure 9-4. Double tight end unbalanced

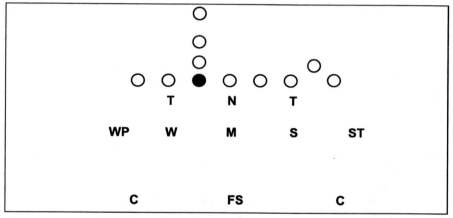

Figure 9-5. Double tight end overload

Defending Specific Power Plays

Defending Double Tight—Blast (Figure 9-6)

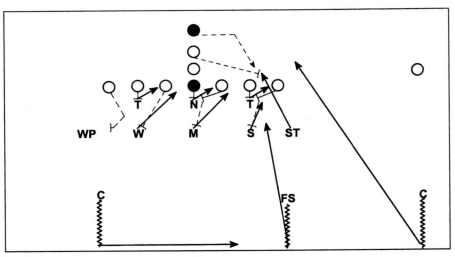

Figure 9-6

Position	Read	Fit
Strong tackle	Slant strong	Strong C gap
Weak tackle	Slant strong	Weak B gap
Nose	Slant strong	Strong A gap
Will	Scoop—flow away	Backside A gap
Mike	Double-team—flow strong	Under the double by the guard if possible—playside B gap
Sam	Double-team—flow strong	Playside D gap—under the down block by the tight end
Whip	Scoop—flow away	Hold and fold
Stud	Down by tight end—flow to	Run the feet of the tight end up the field—take on the fullback with the inside arm—force the play inside
Strong corner	Down—flow to	Secondary force
Weak corner	Scoop—flow away	Roll to post
Free safety	Down—run	Run alley to strongside

Defending Double Tight—Toss Sweep (Figure 9-7)

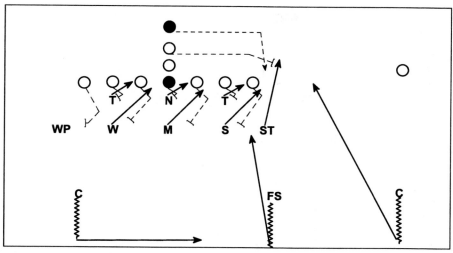

Figure 9-7

Position	Read	Fit
Strong tackle	Slant strong	Strong C gap
Weak tackle	Slant strong	Weak B gap
Nose	Slant strong	Strong A gap
Will	Scoop—flow away	Backside A gap
Mike	Reach—flow strong	Under the reach block by the guard if possible—playside B gap
Sam	Reach—flow strong	Playside D gap—under reach block by the tight end
Whip	Scoop—flow away	Hold and fold
Stud	Reach—flow to	Reach by tight end—beat the tight end up the field—take on the fullback with the inside arm—force the play inside
Strong corner	Reach—flow to	Secondary force
Weak corner	Scoop—flow away	Roll to post
Free safety	Reach—run	Run alley to strongside

Defending Double Tight—Double Wing Blast (Figure 9-8)

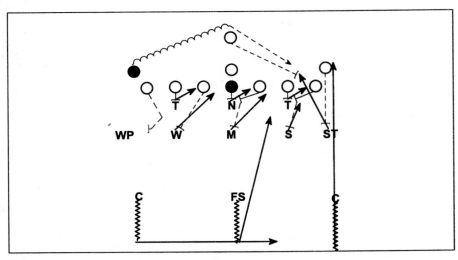

Figure 9-8

Position	Read	Fit
Strong tackle	Slant strong	Strong C gap
Weak tackle	Slant strong	Weak B gap
Nose	Slant strong	Strong A gap
Will	Scoop—flow away	Backside A gap
Mike	Double-team—flow strong	Under the double by the guard if possible—playside B gap
Sam	Double-team—flow strong	Playside D gap—under the down block by the tight end
Whip	Scoop—flow away	Hold and fold
Stud	Down by tight end—flow to	Run the feet of the tight end or the wingback up the field—take on the fullback with the inside arm—force the play inside
Strong corner	Down—flow to	Secondary force
Weak corner	Scoop—flow away	Roll to post
Free safety	Down—run	Run alley to strongside

Defending Double Tight—Double Wing Wingback Lead (Figure 9-9)

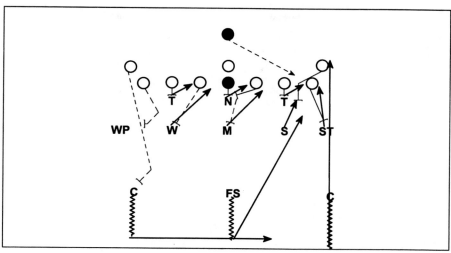

Figure 9-9

Position	Read	Fit
Strong tackle	Slant strong	Strong C gap
Weak tackle	Slant strong	Weak B gap
Nose	Slant strong	Strong A gap
Will	Scoop—flow away	Backside A gap
Mike	Double-team—flow strong	Under the down block by the guard if possible—playside B gap
Sam	Reach base—flow tight	Playside C gap—take on the wingback with the outside arm
Whip	Scoop—flow away	Hold and fold
Stud	Fan—flow to	Beat the tight end up the field—force the play inside
Strong corner	Reach—flow to	Secondary force
Weak corner	Scoop—flow away	Roll to post
Free safety	Down—run	Run alley to strongside

Defending Double Tight—Double Wing Wingback Counter (Figure 9-10)

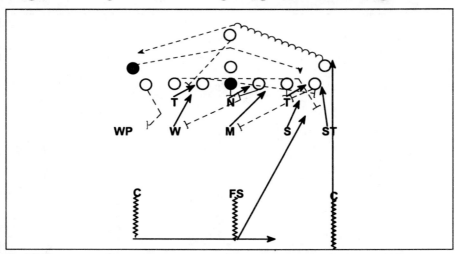

Figure 9-10

Position	Read	Fit
Strong tackle	Slant strong	Strong C gap
Weak tackle	Slant strong	Weak B gap
Nose	Slant strong	Strong A gap
Will	Pull—flow away	Backside A gap—take the fullback
Mike	Double-team—flow weak	Under the down block by the tight end if possible—playside B gap
Sam	Double-team—flow weak	Playside C gap—take on the pulling tackle with the outside arm
Whip	Scoop—flow away	Hold and fold
Stud	Down—flow away	Run the feet of the tight end up the field—take on the pulling guard with the inside arm—force the play inside
Strong corner	Reach—flow to	Secondary force
Weak corner	Scoop—flow away	Roll to post
Free safety	Down—run	Run alley to strongside

Other Options Versus Power Formations

Tuff (Figure 9-11)—Versus double tight, it may be helpful to bring the Stud linebacker down as a fourth defensive lineman and play the tuff front.

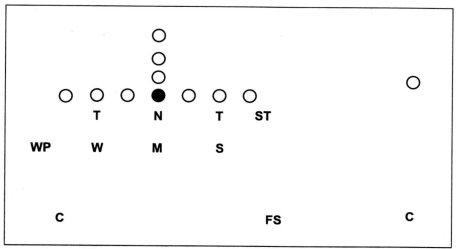

Figure 9-11. Tuff versus double tight

Goal line (Figures 9-12 and 9-13)—In short-yardage situations, it is sometimes helpful to jump into goal line to add extra defenders to the line of scrimmage.

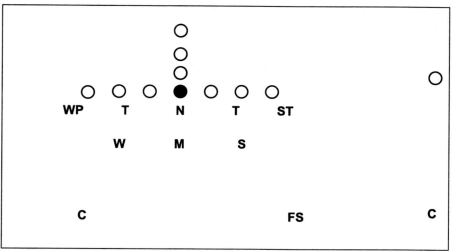

Figure 9-12. Goal line versus double tight

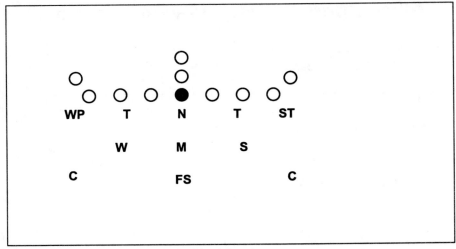

Figure 9-13. Goal line versus double tight wing

Defending Against the Option

Because the defensive front is always slanting either right or left, the option rules will change depending on the direction of the slant and the type of option being run. This defensive system does have a base set of option responsibilities in place. As stated earlier, they can and will change. The defenders' responsibilities are as follows:

- Tackles—If slanting in, tackles take the dive. If slanting out, they take the quarterback.
- Nose—Dive
- Mike—Dive
- Sam and Will—Responsibilities are opposite those of the tackles. If the tackle slants out, Sam and Will take the dive. If the tackle slants in, Sam and Will take the quarterback.
- Stud and Whip—Straight to the pitch
- Free safety—Quarterback to pitch
- Corners—Pitch (late)

Slant Strong Versus Inside Veer (Figure 9-14)

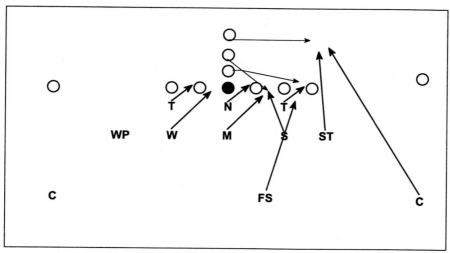

Figure 9-14

Position	Fit
Strong tackle	Quarterback
Weak tackle	Dive
Nose	Dive
Will	Backside A
Mike	Dive
Sam	Tackle
Whip	Hold and fold
Stud	Pitch
Strong corner	Pitch
Weak corner	Roll to post
Free safety	Quarterback to pitch

Slant Weak Versus Inside Veer (Figure 9-15)

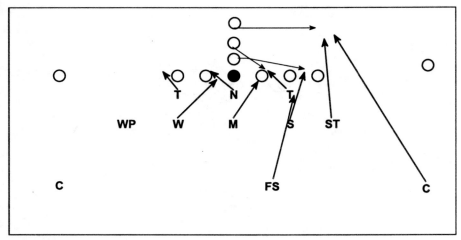

Figure 9-15

Position	Fit
Strong tackle	Dive
Weak tackle	Dive
Nose	Dive
Will	Backside A
Mike	Dive
Sam	Quarterback
Whip	Hold and fold
Stud	Pitch
Strong corner	Pitch
Weak corner	Roll to post
Free safety	Quarterback to pitch

In Versus Inside Veer (Figure 9-16)

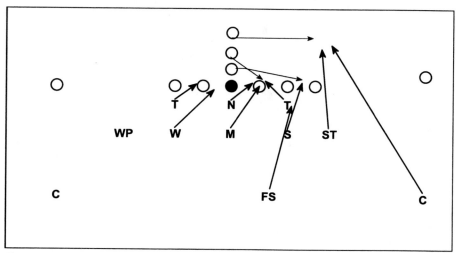

Figure 9-16

Position	Fit
Strong tackle	Dive
Weak tackle	Dive
Nose	Dive
Will	Backside A
Mike	Dive
Sam	Quarterback
Whip	Hold and fold
Stud	Pitch
Strong corner	Pitch
Weak corner	Roll to post
Free safety	Quarterback to pitch

Out Versus Inside Veer (Figure 9-17)

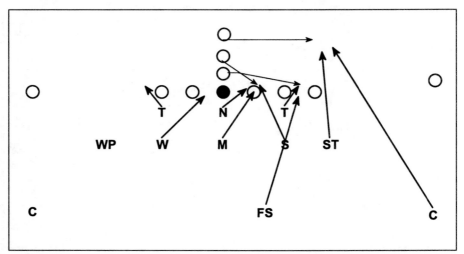

Figure 9-17

Position	Fit
Strong tackle	Quarterback
Weak tackle	Dive
Nose	Dive
Will	Backside A
Mike	Dive
Sam	Dive
Whip	Hold and fold
Stud	Pitch
Strong corner	Pitch
Weak corner	Roll to post
Free safety	Quarterback to pitch

Pinch Versus Inside Veer (Figure 9-18)

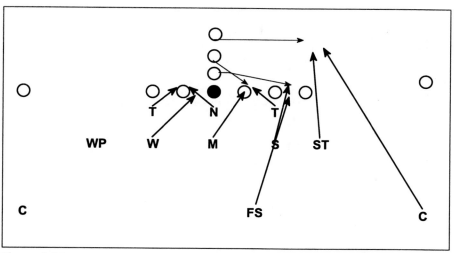

Figure 9-18

Position	Fit
Strong tackle	Dive
Weak tackle	Dive
Nose	Dive
Will	Backside A
Mike	Dive
Sam	Quarterback
Whip	Hold and fold
Stud	Pitch
Strong corner	Pitch
Weak corner	Roll to post
Free safety	Quarterback to pitch

Slant Strong Versus Outside Veer (Figure 9-19)

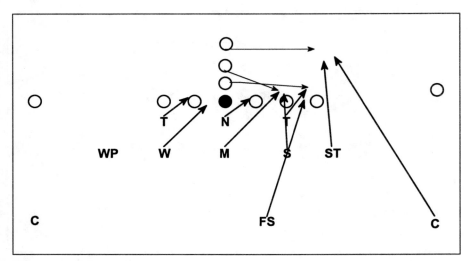

Figure 9-19

Position	Fit
Strong tackle	Quarterback
Weak tackle	Dive
Nose	Dive
Will	Backside A
Mike	Dive
Sam	Tackle
Whip	Hold and fold
Stud	Pitch
Strong corner	Pitch
Weak corner	Roll to post
Free safety	Quarterback to pitch

Slant Weak Versus Outside Veer (Figure 9-20)

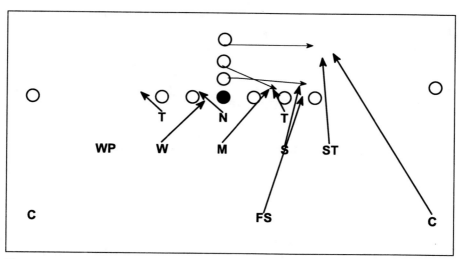

Figure 9-20

Position	Fit
Strong tackle	Dive
Weak tackle	Dive
Nose	Dive
Will	Backside A
Mike	Dive
Sam	Quarterback
Whip	Hold and fold
Stud	Pitch
Strong corner	Pitch
Weak corner	Roll to post
Free safety	Quarterback to pitch

In Versus Outside Veer (Figure 9-21)

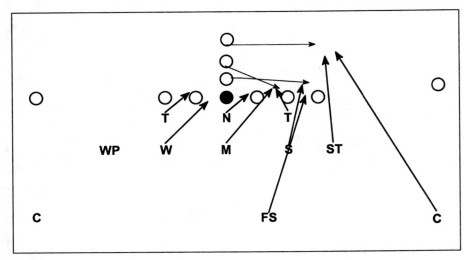

Figure 9-21

Position	Fit
Strong tackle	Dive
Weak tackle	Dive
Nose	Dive
Will	Backside A
Mike	Dive
Sam	Quarterback
Whip	Hold and fold
Stud	Pitch
Strong corner	Pitch
Weak corner	Roll to post
Free safety	Quarterback to pitch

Out Versus Outside Veer (Figure 9-22)

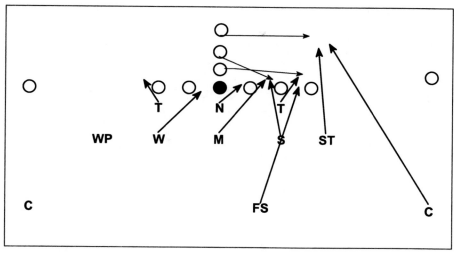

Figure 9-22

Position	Fit
Strong tackle	Quarterback
Weak tackle	Dive
Nose	Dive
Will	Backside A
Mike	Dive
Sam	Dive
Whip	Hold and fold
Stud	Pitch
Strong corner	Pitch
Weak corner	Roll to post
Free safety	Quarterback to pitch

Pinch Versus Outside Veer (Figure 9-23)

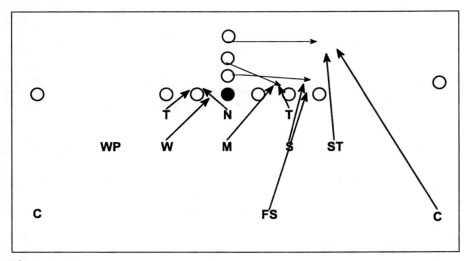

Figure 9-23

Position	Fit
Strong tackle	Dive
Weak tackle	Dive
Nose	Dive
Will	Backside A
Mike	Dive
Sam	Quarterback
Whip	Hold and fold
Stud	Pitch
Strong corner	Pitch
Weak corner	Roll to post
Free safety	Quarterback to pitch

Slant Strong Versus Midline (Figure 9-24)

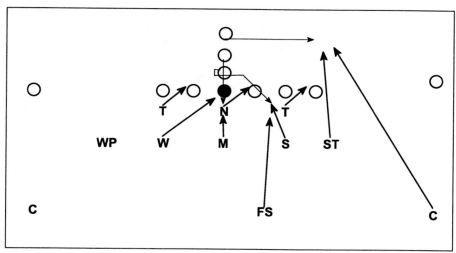

Figure 9-24

Position	Fit
Strong tackle	Quarterback
Weak tackle	Dive
Nose	Dive
Will	Backside A
Mike	Dive
Sam	Tackle
Whip	Hold and fold
Stud	Pitch
Strong corner	Pitch
Weak corner	Roll to post
Free safety	Quarterback to pitch

Slant Weak Versus Midline (Figure 9-25)

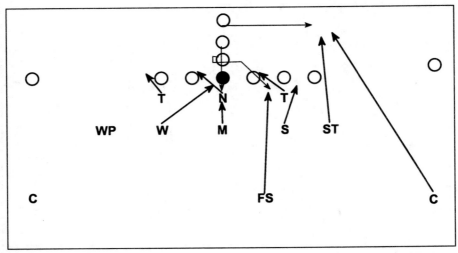

Figure 9-25

Position	Fit
Strong tackle	Dive
Weak tackle	Dive
Nose	Dive
Will	Backside A
Mike	Dive
Sam	Quarterback
Whip	Hold and fold
Stud	Pitch
Strong corner	Pitch
Weak corner	Roll to post
Free safety	Quarterback to pitch

In Versus Midline (Figure 9-26)

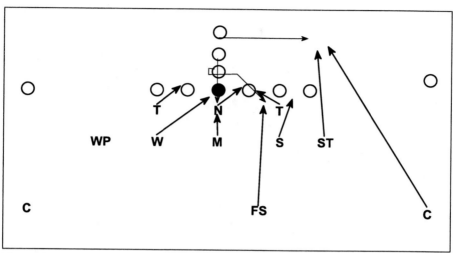

Figure 9-26

Position	Fit
Strong tackle	Dive
Weak tackle	Dive
Nose	Dive
Will	Backside A
Mike	Dive
Sam	Quarterback
Whip	Hold and fold
Stud	Pitch
Strong corner	Pitch
Weak corner	Roll to post
Free safety	Quarterback to pitch

Out Versus Midline (Figure 9-27)

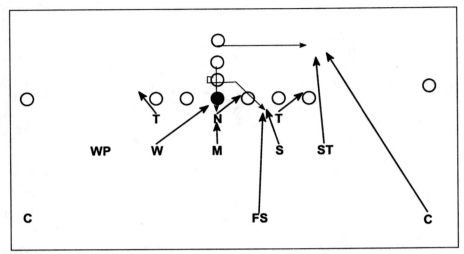

Figure 9-27

Position	Fit
Strong tackle	Quarterback
Weak tackle	Dive
Nose	Dive
Will	Backside A
Mike	Dive
Sam	Dive
Whip	Hold and fold
Stud	Pitch
Strong corner	Pitch
Weak corner	Roll to post
Free safety	Quarterback to pitch

Pinch Versus Midline (Figure 9-28)

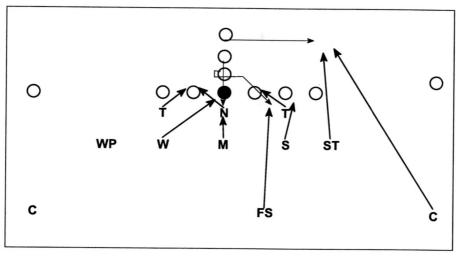

Figure 9-28

Position	Fit
Strong tackle	Dive
Weak tackle	Dive
Nose	Dive
Will	Backside A
Mike	Dive
Sam	Quarterback
Whip	Hold and fold
Stud	Pitch
Strong corner	Pitch
Weak corner	Roll to post
Free safety	Quarterback to pitch

Slant Strong Versus Speed Option (Figure 9-29)

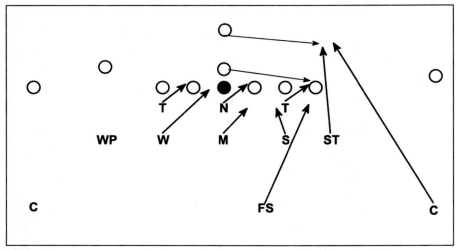

Figure 9-29

Position	Fit
Strong tackle	Quarterback
Weak tackle	Fit
Nose	Fit
Will	Backside A
Mike	Fit
Sam	Fit
Whip	Hold and fold
Stud	Pitch
Strong corner	Pitch
Weak corner	Roll to post
Free safety	Quarterback to pitch

Slant Weak Versus Speed Option (Figure 9-30)

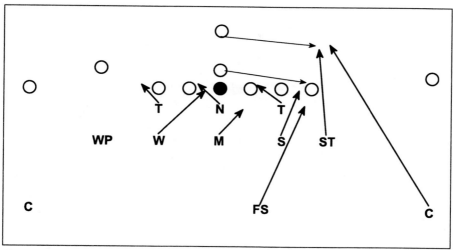

Figure 9-30

Position	Fit
Strong tackle	Fit
Weak tackle	Fit
Nose	Fit
Will	Backside A
Mike	Fit
Sam	Quarterback
Whip	Hold and fold
Stud	Pitch
Strong corner	Pitch
Weak corner	Roll to post
Free safety	Quarterback to pitch

In Versus Speed Option (Figure 9-31)

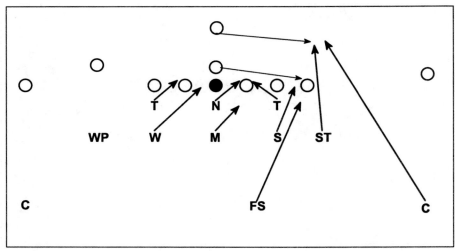

Figure 9-31

Position	Fit
Strong tackle	Fit
Weak tackle	Fit
Nose	Fit
Will	Backside A
Mike	Fit
Sam	Quarterback
Whip	Hold and fold
Stud	Pitch
Strong corner	Pitch
Weak corner	Roll to post
Free safety	Quarterback to pitch

Out Versus Speed Option (Figure 9-32)

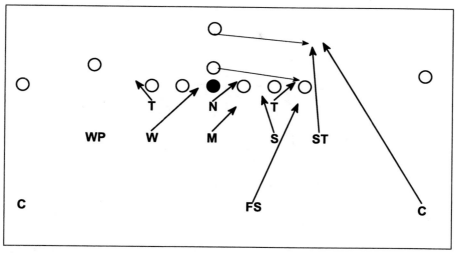

Figure 9-32

Position	Fit
Strong tackle	Quarterback
Weak tackle	Fit
Nose	Fit
Will	Backside A
Mike	Fit
Sam	Fit
Whip	Hold and fold
Stud	Pitch
Strong corner	Pitch
Weak corner	Roll to post
Free safety	Quarterback to pitch

Pinch Versus Speed Option (Figure 9-33)

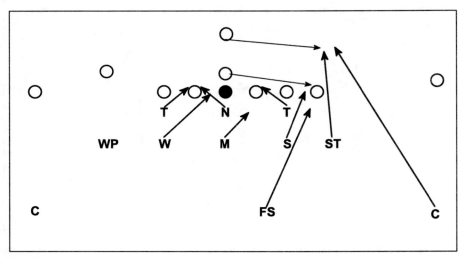

Figure 9-33

Position	Fit
Strong tackle	Fit
Weak tackle	Fit
Nose	Fit
Will	Backside A
Mike	Fit
Sam	Quarterback
Whip	Hold and fold
Stud	Pitch
Strong corner	Pitch
Weak corner	Roll to post
Free safety	Quarterback to pitch

Effective Blitzes Versus the Option
(Figures 9-34 through 9-36)

This defensive scheme is capable of forcing offenses out of the option through the use of pressures that take away the dive and quarterback at the mesh point. The key point in playing the option is for the defense to try and turn every play into a toss sweep as quickly as they can, which can only be accomplished by attacking the mesh between the quarterback and fullback. Attacking the mesh is the focal point in defending against the option with the 3-5-3 defense.

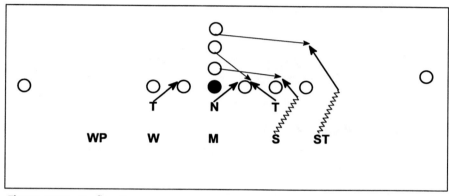

Figure 9-34. In, fire, Sam go

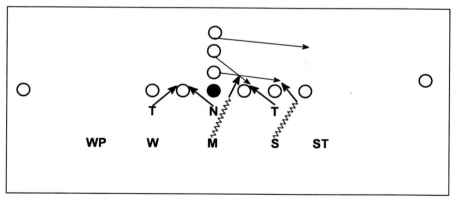

Figure 9-35. Pinch, dog strong

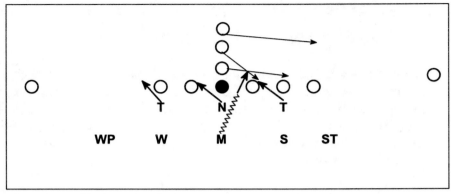

Figure 9-36. Slant weak, Mike go

Defending Against the Double-Slot Option

Double-slot formations create the following problems for the defense:

- Four vertical pass threats exist on every play.
- The positions of the slots allow for angles to down block the defensive tackles.
- Due to the nature of the formation, misdirection is common.
- The placement of the fullback makes quick-hitting plays a problem.
- This formation is very conducive to running the option.

Defenses must adhere to the following guidelines when facing a double-slot formation:

- Always honor the four vertical threats.
- Keep the outside linebackers outside of the slots to prevent them from getting blocked down on.
- Stay at home backside to take care of misdirection.
- Do not get outflanked by motion.
- Be disciplined and play the option responsibilities correctly.

Slant Strong Versus Double-Slot Inside Veer (Figure 9-37)

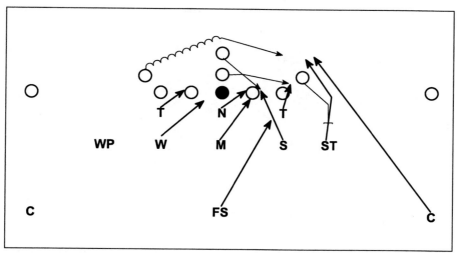

Figure 9-37

Position	Fit
Strong tackle	Quarterback
Weak tackle	Dive
Nose	Dive
Will	Backside A
Mike	Dive
Sam	Tackle
Whip	Hold and fold
Stud	Pitch
Strong corner	Pitch
Weak corner	Roll to post
Free safety	Quarterback to pitch

Slant Weak Versus Double-Slot Inside Veer (Figure 9-38)

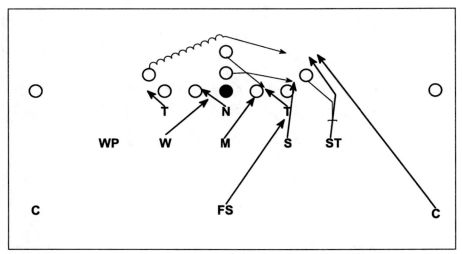

Figure 9-38

Position	Fit
Strong tackle	Dive
Weak tackle	Dive
Nose	Dive
Will	Backside A
Mike	Dive
Sam	Quarterback
Whip	Hold and fold
Stud	Pitch
Strong corner	Pitch
Weak corner	Roll to post
Free safety	Quarterback to pitch

In Versus Double-Slot Inside Veer (Figure 9-39)

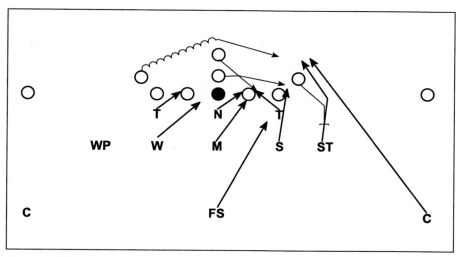

Figure 9-39

Position	Fit
Strong tackle	Dive
Weak tackle	Dive
Nose	Dive
Will	Backside A
Mike	Dive
Sam	Quarterback
Whip	Hold and fold
Stud	Pitch
Strong corner	Pitch
Weak corner	Roll to post
Free safety	Quarterback to pitch

Out Versus Double-Slot Inside Veer (Figure 9-40)

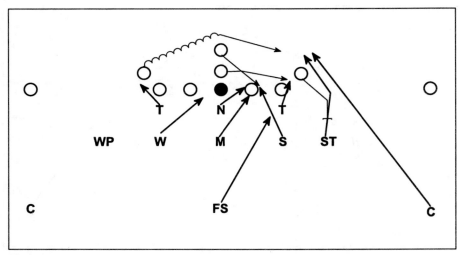

Figure 9-40

Position	Fit
Strong tackle	Quarterback
Weak tackle	Dive
Nose	Dive
Will	Backside A
Mike	Dive
Sam	Dive
Whip	Hold and fold
Stud	Pitch
Strong corner	Pitch
Weak corner	Roll to post
Free safety	Quarterback to pitch

Pinch Versus Double-Slot Inside Veer (Figure 9-41)

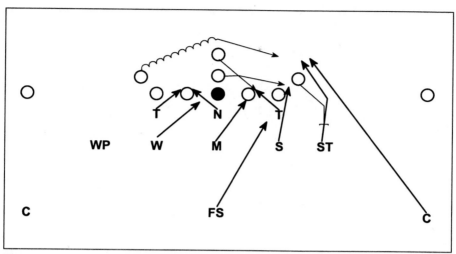

Figure 9-41

Position	Fit
Strong tackle	Dive
Weak tackle	Dive
Nose	Dive
Will	Backside A
Mike	Dive
Sam	Quarterback
Whip	Hold and fold
Stud	Pitch
Strong corner	Pitch
Weak corner	Roll to post
Free safety	Quarterback to pitch

Slant Strong Versus Double-Slot Midline (Figure 9-42)

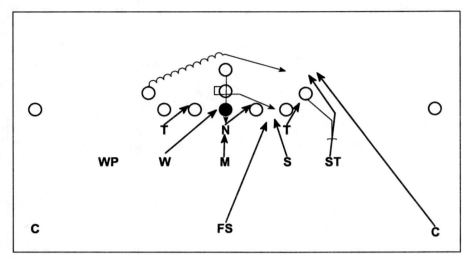

Figure 9-42

Position	Fit
Strong tackle	Quarterback
Weak tackle	Dive
Nose	Dive
Will	Backside A
Mike	Dive
Sam	Tackle
Whip	Hold and fold
Stud	Pitch
Strong corner	Pitch
Weak corner	Roll to post
Free safety	Quarterback to pitch

Slant Weak Versus Double-Slot Midline (Figure 9-43)

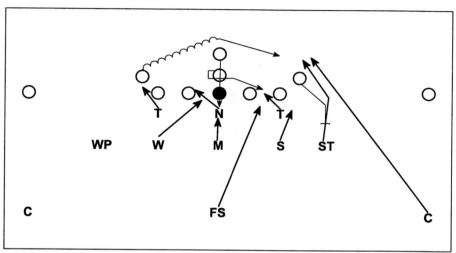

Figure 9-43

Position	Fit
Strong tackle	Dive
Weak tackle	Dive
Nose	Dive
Will	Backside A
Mike	Dive
Sam	Quarterback
Whip	Hold and fold
Stud	Pitch
Strong corner	Pitch
Weak corner	Roll to post
Free safety	Quarterback to pitch

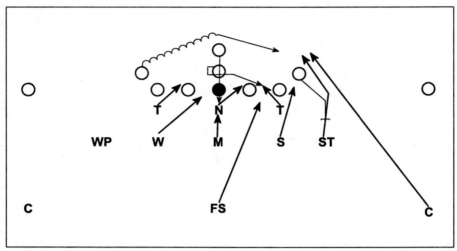

Figure 9-44

Position	Fit
Strong tackle	Dive
Weak tackle	Dive
Nose	Dive
Will	Backside A
Mike	Dive
Sam	Quarterback
Whip	Hold and fold
Stud	Pitch
Strong corner	Pitch
Weak corner	Roll to post
Free safety	Quarterback to pitch

Out Versus Double-Slot Midline (Figure 9-45)

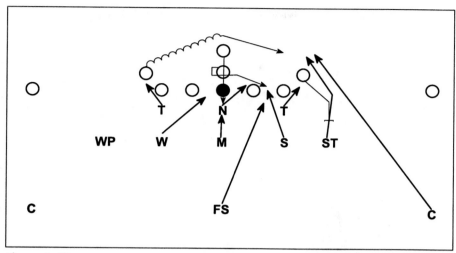

Figure 9-45

Position	Fit
Strong tackle	Quarterback
Weak tackle	Dive
Nose	Dive
Will	Backside A
Mike	Dive
Sam	Dive
Whip	Hold and fold
Stud	Pitch
Strong corner	Pitch
Weak corner	Roll to post
Free safety	Quarterback to pitch

Pinch Versus Double-Slot Midline (Figure 9-46)

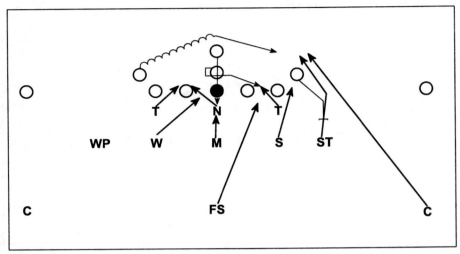

Figure 9-46

Position	Fit
Strong tackle	Dive
Weak tackle	Dive
Nose	Dive
Will	Backside A
Mike	Dive
Sam	Quarterback
Whip	Hold and fold
Stud	Pitch
Strong corner	Pitch
Weak corner	Roll to post
Free safety	Quarterback to pitch

Defending Against the
Spread Offense

Teams running the spread try to accomplish the following versus your defense:

- Get you to remove linebackers from the box and lose gap integrity.
- Rub or mesh your defensive backs when you are in man coverage.
- Find holes in your zone coverage.
- Get you thinking pass and bust you with the run.
- Pick up your blitzes and give the quarterback time to throw.
- Reduce outside pressure by making your outside linebackers cover receivers.

A 3-5-3 defense should try to do the following when facing teams running the spread:

- Force the quarterback to throw under distress.
- Maintain gap integrity.
- Confuse the quarterback by disguising and changing coverages.
- Force the quarterback to try and find the holes in the zone coverage.
- Shut down the run by maintaining gap integrity, thereby making the offense one-dimensional.

Coaches who run the 3-5-3 defense should hold the following beliefs:

- The defense will dictate to the offense what they can and cannot run.
- The defense wants to send as much pressure as possible and keep the offense off-balance.
- The defense wants the offense waiting to see what will happen next.
- The defense will void zones in zone coverage and force the offense to find the holes under pressure.

Terminology

Sky—This call tells the defense that they are showing cover 3, but rolling to cover 4 with the Whip and free safety. The Will inside linebacker has hook/curl/flats weak.

Banjo—This call means that an outside linebacker is called on to blitz, but is responsible for a player in man coverage. The outside linebacker will call "banjo" to either tell the free safety to take his man or banjo the blitz to the inside linebacker to perform.

Cat—Tells the Will linebacker to slide out to four yards by four yards

Cover 1—Man free coverage. The defense is man underneath and the free safety is playing center field.

Cover 4—True quarters coverage

Cover 3—Three deep zone coverage

Man—True man-to-man coverage

Coverages (Figures 10-1 through 10-6)

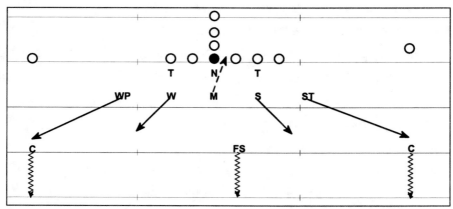

Figure 10-1. Cover 3

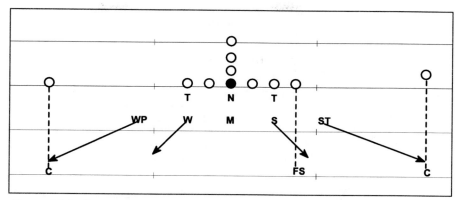

Figure 10-2. Cover man

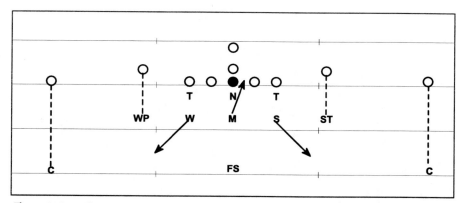

Figure 10-3. Cover 1

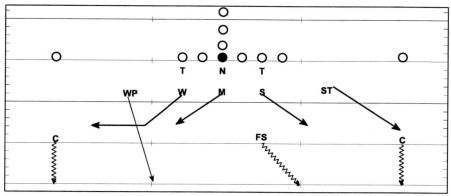

Figure 10-4. Cover 3 sky

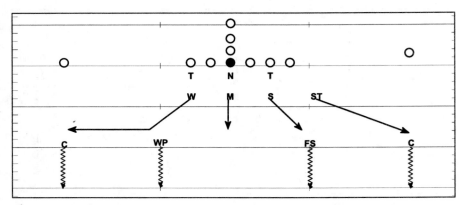

Figure 10-5. Cover 4

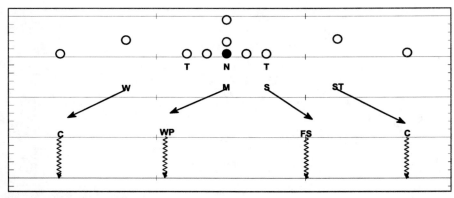

Figure 10-6. Cat cover 4

Formation Adjustments Against the Spread (Figures 10-7 through 10-22)

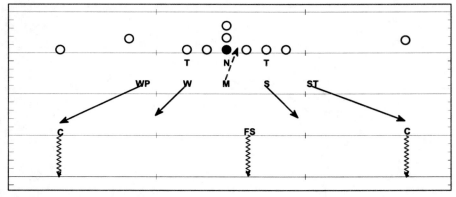

Figure 10-7. Pro twins (option 1: stay in 3)

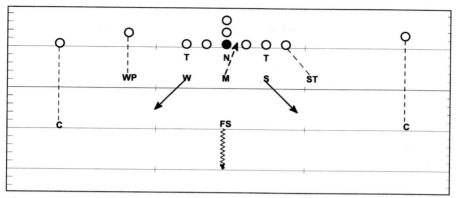

Figure 10-8. Pro twins [option 2: check to 1(man free)]

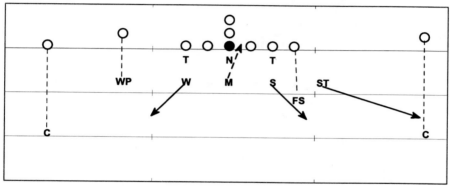

Figure 10-9. Pro twins (option 3: check to man)

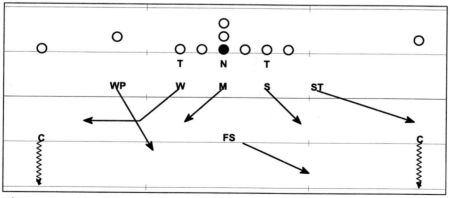

Figure 10-10. Pro twins [option 4: roll to 4 (sky)]

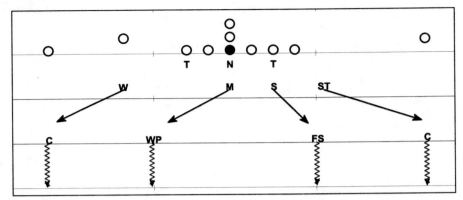

Figure 10-11. Pro twins (option 5: check to cat cover 4)

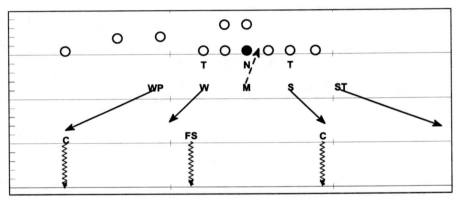

Figure 10-12. Shotgun spread trips (option 1: stay in 3)

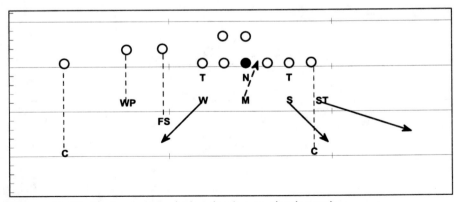

Figure 10-13. Shotgun spread trips (option 2: check man)

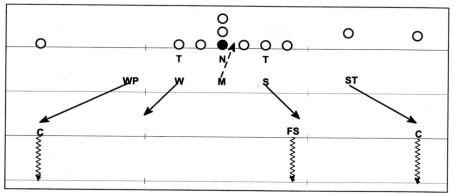

Figure 10-14. Shotgun spread trio (option 1: stay in 3)

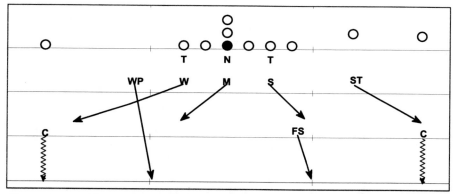

Figure 10-15. Shotgun spread trio [option 2: roll to 4 (sky)]

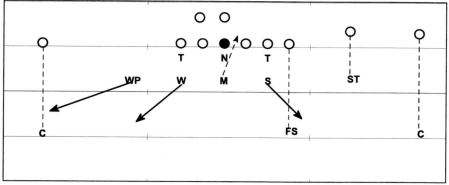

Figure 10-16. Shotgun spread trio [option 3: 1 (man free)]

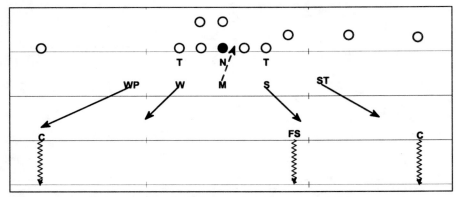

Figure 10-17. Shotgun spread trips open (option 1: stay in 3)

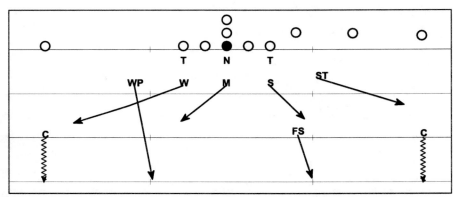

Figure 10-18. Shotgun spread trips open [option 2: roll to 4 (sky)]

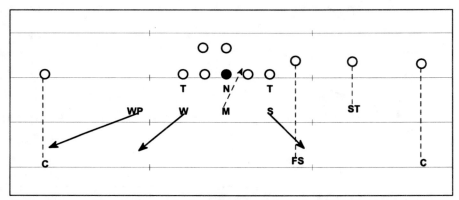

Figure 10-19. Shotgun spread trips open [option 3: 1 (man free)]

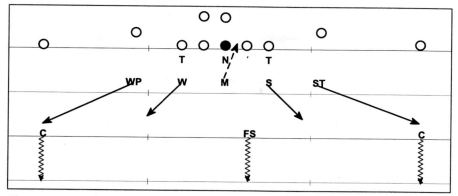

Figure 10-20. Shotgun spread double twins (option 1: stay in 3)

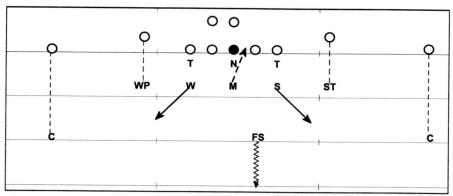

Figure 10-21. Shotgun spread double twins [option 2: check 1 (man free)]

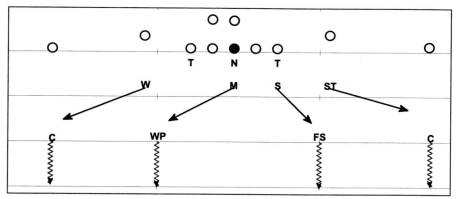

Figure 10-22. Shotgun spread double twins (option 3: check to cat cover 4)

Defending Empty Sets (Figures 10-23 through 10-29)

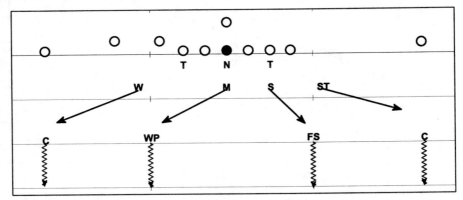

Figure 10-23. Shotgun spread empty pro trips—check to cat cover 4

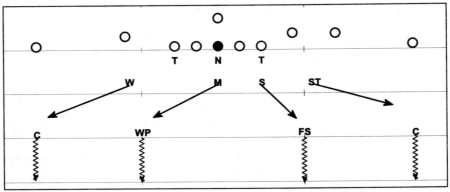

Figure 10-24. Shotgun spread empty trips twins—check to cat cover 4

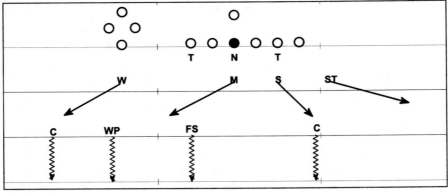

Figure 10-25. Shotgun spread empty quads—check to cat cover 4

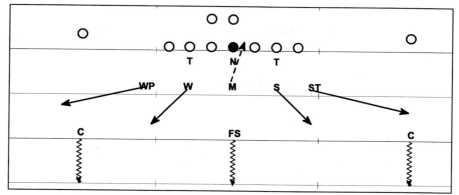

Figure 10-26. Shotgun spread moose (option 1: stay in 3)

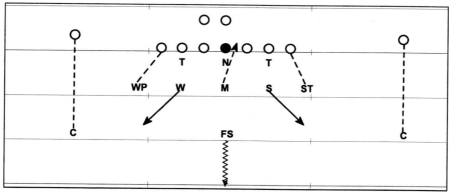

Figure 10-27. Shotgun spread moose [option 2: check to cover 1 (man free)]

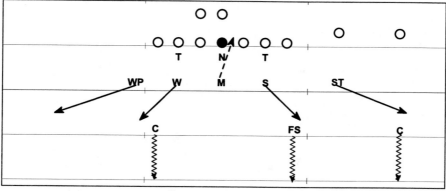

Figure 10-28. Shotgun spread moose-trio (option 1: stay in 3)

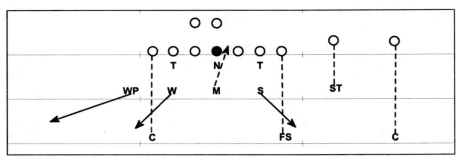

Figure 10-29. Shotgun spread moose-trio [option 2: check to cover 1(man free)]

Motion Adjustments

- When in doubt, check to cover 3 and play football.
- Cover 4 (quarters) is the "emergency" coverage that is used when the offense shows something spread but unexpected.

Defending the Run

Zone (Figure 10-30)

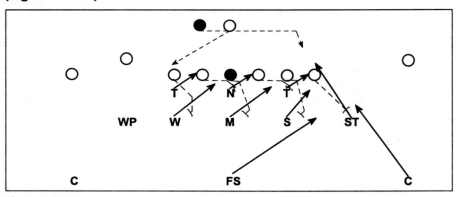

Figure 10-30

Position	Read	Fit
Strong tackle	Slant strong	Strong C gap
Weak tackle	Slant strong	Weak B gap
Nose	Slant strong	Strong A gap
Will	Scoop—flow away	Backside A gap
Mike	Double-team—flow strong	Under double by the guard if possible—playside B gap
Sam	Double-team—flow strong	Step to outside of the double-team—refit under because of flow
Whip	Scoop—flow away	Hold and fold
Stud	Down by tight end—flow to	Run the feet of the tight end up the field—force the play inside
Strong corner	Down—flow to	Secondary force
Weak corner	Scoop—flow away	Roll to post
Free safety	Down—run	Run alley to strongside

Sweep (Figure 10-31)

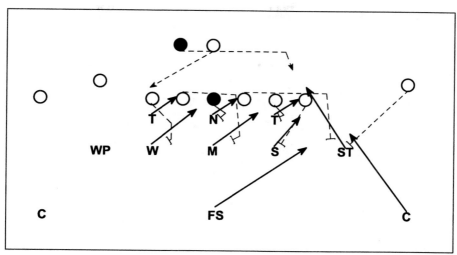

Figure 10-31

Position	Read	Fit
Strong tackle	Slant strong	Strong C gap
Weak tackle	Slant strong	Weak B gap
Nose	Slant strong	Strong A gap
Will	Scoop—flow away	Backside A gap
Mike	Reach—flow strong	Under the pulling guard—playside B gap
Sam	Reach—flow strong	Playside C gap—under the pulling guard or the down block by the tight end
Whip	Scoop—flow away	Hold and fold
Stud	Down by tight end—flow to	Run the feet of the tight end up the field—force the play inside
Strong corner	Down—flow to	Secondary force
Weak corner	Scoop—flow away	Roll to post
Free safety	Down—run	Run alley to strongside

Trap (Figure 10-32)

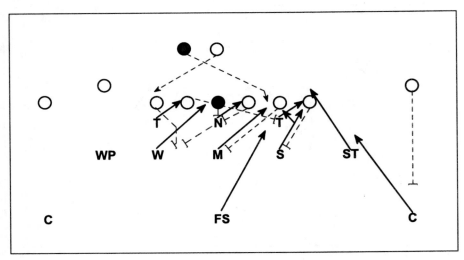

Figure 10-32

Position	Read	Fit
Strong tackle	Slant strong	Strong C gap
Weak tackle	Slant strong	Weak B gap
Nose	Slant strong	Strong A gap
Will	Scoop—flow away	Backside A gap
Mike	Base/double-team—flow strong	Fit under the down block by the tackle if possible—playside B gap
Sam	Down—flow inside	Playside C gap—under the down block by the tight end
Whip	Scoop—flow away	Hold and fold
Stud	Down by tight end—flow to	Run the feet of the tight end up the field—force the play inside
Strong corner	Down—flow to	Secondary force
Weak corner	Scoop—flow away	Roll to post
Free safety	Down—run	Run alley to strongside

Lead (Figure 10-33)

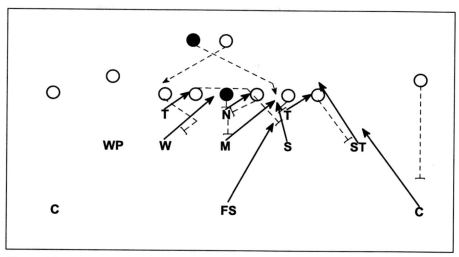

Figure 10-33

Position	Read	Fit
Strong tackle	Slant strong	Strong C gap
Weak tackle	Slant strong	Weak B gap
Nose	Slant strong	Strong A gap
Will	Scoop—flow away	Backside A gap
Mike	Base/double-team—flow strong	Fit under the down block by the tackle if possible—playside B gap
Sam	Fan—flow inside	Fill the open window—take on the guard with the outside arm and make the ball bounce
Whip	Scoop—flow away	Hold and fold
Stud	Fan by tight end—flow to	Beat the tight end up the field—force the play inside
Strong corner	Fan—flow to	Secondary force
Weak corner	Scoop—flow away	Roll to post
Free safety	Fan—run	Run alley to strongside

Power (Figure 10-34)

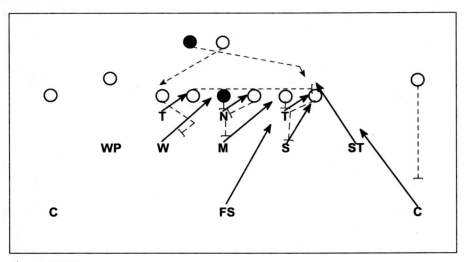

Figure 10-34

Position	Read	Fit
Strong tackle	Slant strong	Strong C gap
Weak tackle	Slant strong	Weak B gap
Nose	Slant strong	Strong A gap
Will	Scoop—flow away	Backside A gap
Mike	Base/double-team—flow strong	Fit under the down block by the tackle if possible—playside B gap
Sam	Base/double-team—flow outside	Under the chip by the tackle—playside C gap
Whip	Scoop—flow away	Hold and fold
Stud	Down by tight end—flow to	Run the feet of the tight end into the D gap—force the play inside
Strong corner	Down—flow to	Secondary force
Weak corner	Scoop—flow away	Roll to post
Free safety	Down—run	Run alley to strongside

Effective Blitzes Against the Spread

Three to the Weakside (Figures 10-35 through 10-38)

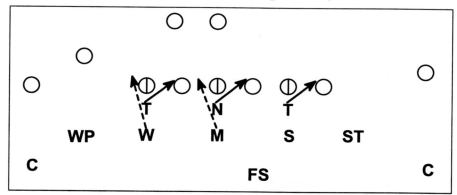

Figure 10-35. Slant strong, dog weak

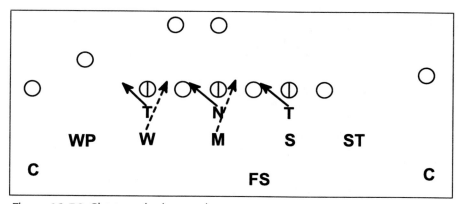

Figure 10-36. Slant weak, dog weak

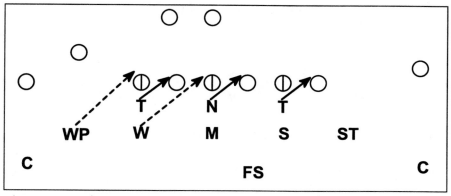

Figure 10-37. Slant strong, Will A, Whip fire

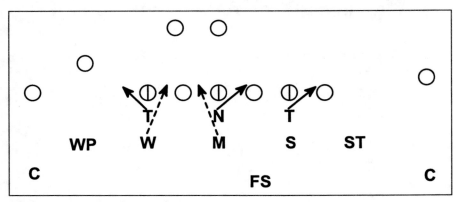

Figure 10-38. Out, dog weak

Three to the Strongside (Figures 10-39 and 10-40)

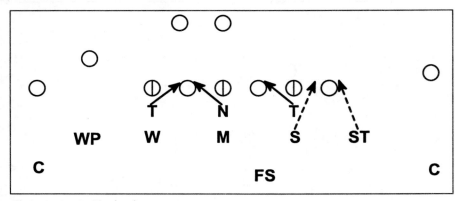

Figure 10-39. Pinch, dog strong

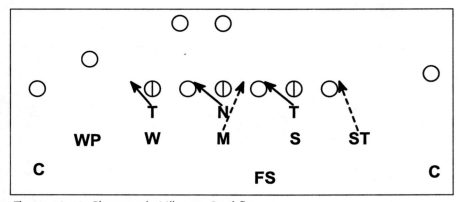

Figure 10-40. Slant weak, Mike go, Stud fire

Four to the Strongside (Figures 10-41 and 10-42)

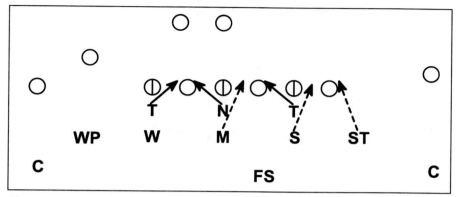

Figure 10-41. Pinch, dog strong, Stud fire

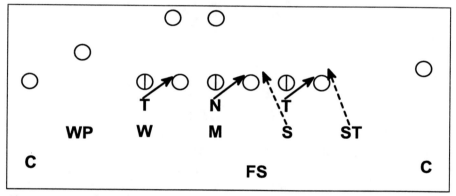

Figure 10-42. Slant strong, Sam go, Stud fire

Conclusion

Success versus the spread is dependant on several things:

- The defense cannot get outflanked by formations.
- The defense must work formation adjustments, motion adjustment, and checks every day.
- All adjustments must be made correctly and in a timely manner.
- The running game must be shut down by the front six players.

11

Defending Against Common Plays

Game Planning

During your game-planning sessions, determine what your opponents do best and what their favorite plays are, and then set out to stop those plays. Times will arise when you may decide to play entire games while only running one front call because that strategy is what you feel gives you the best chance of success. Other times, you may decide to always make the strength call to the field or even to a specific player. All of these tactics are fine, as long as you decide that they are what give you the advantage. The figures that follow illustrate how to defend against some very popular and widely run plays.

I Formation Weakside Counter (Figure 11-1)

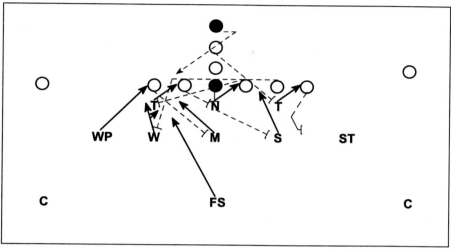

Figure 11-1

Position	Read	Fit
Strong tackle	Slant strong	Strong C gap
Weak tackle	Slant strong	Weak B gap
Nose	Slant strong	Strong A gap
Will	Down—flow to	Outside of the down block—be prepared to redirect back under if flow dictates
Mike	Base/double-team—flow weak	Fit under the down block by the tackle if possible—playside B gap
Sam	Pull—flow away	Backside A gap—take the fullback
Whip	Down—flow to	Run the feet of the tackle and take on any pulling lineman with the inside arm—turn the play inside
Stud	Scoop—flow away	Hold and fold
Strong corner	Scoop—flow away	Roll to post
Weak corner	Down—flow to	Secondary force
Free safety	Fan—run	Run alley to weakside

I Formation Isolation (Figure 11-2)

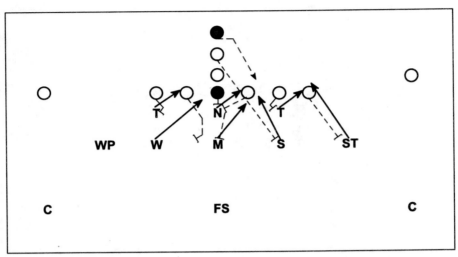

Figure 11-2

Position	Read	Fit
Strong tackle	Slant strong	Strong C gap
Weak tackle	Slant strong	Weak B gap
Nose	Slant strong	Strong A gap
Will	Scoop—flow away	Backside A gap
Mike	Base/double-team—flow strong	Fit under the down block by the tackle if possible—playside B gap
Sam	Fan—flow inside	Fill the open window—take on the fullback with the outside arm and make the ball bounce
Whip	Scoop—flow away	Hold and fold
Stud	Fan by tight end—flow to	Beat the tight end up the field—force the play inside
Strong corner	Fan—flow to	Secondary force
Weak corner	Scoop—flow away	Roll to post
Free safety	Fan—run	Run alley to strongside

I Formation Blast (Figure 11-3)

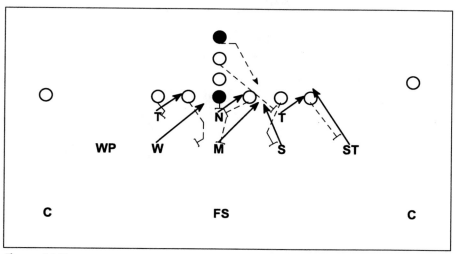

Figure 11-3

Position	Read	Fit
Strong tackle	Slant strong	Strong C gap
Weak tackle	Slant strong	Weak B gap
Nose	Slant strong	Strong A gap
Will	Scoop—flow away	Backside A gap
Mike	Base/double-team—flow strong	Fit under the down block by the tackle if possible—playside B gap
Sam	Inside release—flow inside	Under the inside release by the tackle—playside B gap
Whip	Scoop—flow away	Hold and fold
Stud	Fan by tight end—flow to	Beat the tight end up the field—force the play inside
Strong corner	Fan—flow to	Secondary force
Weak corner	Scoop—flow away	Roll to post
Free safety	Fan—run	Run alley to strongside

Spread Zone (Figure 11-4)

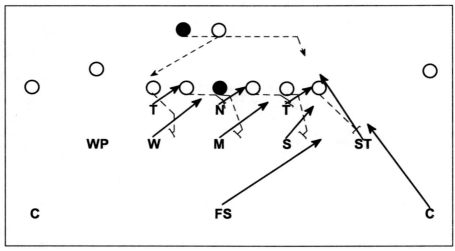

Figure 11-4

Position	Read	Fit
Strong tackle	Slant strong	Strong C gap
Weak tackle	Slant strong	Weak B gap
Nose	Slant strong	Strong A gap
Will	Scoop—flow away	Backside A gap
Mike	Double-team—flow strong	Under the double by the guard if possible—playside B gap
Sam	Double-team—flow strong	Step to the outside of the double-team—refit under because of flow
Whip	Scoop—flow away	Hold and fold
Stud	Down by Tight end—flow to	Run the feet of the tight end up the field—force the play inside
Strong corner	Down—flow to	Secondary force
Weak corner	Scoop—flow away	Roll to post
Free safety	Down—run	Run alley to strongside

Spread trap (Figure 11-5)

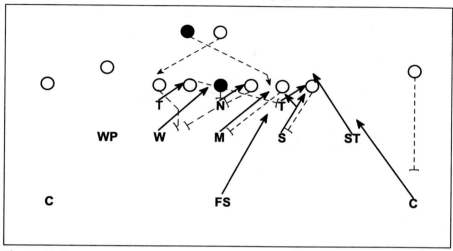

Figure 11-5

Position	Read	Fit
Strong tackle	Slant strong	Strong C gap
Weak tackle	Slant strong	Weak B gap
Nose	Slant strong	Strong A gap
Will	Scoop—flow away	Backside A gap
Mike	Base/double-team—flow strong	Fit under the down block by the tackle if possible—playside B gap
Sam	Down—flow inside	Playside C gap—under the down block by the tight end
Whip	Scoop—flow away	Hold and fold
Stud	Down by tight end—flow to	Run the feet of the tight end up the field—force the play inside
Strong corner	Down—flow to	Secondary force
Weak corner	Scoop—flow away	Roll to post
Free safety	Down—run	Run alley to strongside

Wing T Buck Sweep (Figure 11-6)

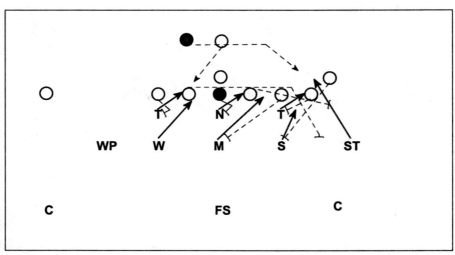

Figure 11-6

Position	Read	Fit
Strong tackle	Slant strong	Strong C gap
Weak tackle	Slant strong	Weak B gap
Nose	Slant strong	Strong A gap
Will	Scoop—flow away	Backside A gap—take fullback
Mike	Reach—flow strong	Fit under the down block by the tackle if possible—playside B gap
Sam	Down—flow to	Playside C gap—under the down block by the tight end or wingback
Whip	Scoop—flow away	Hold and fold
Stud	Down by tight end—flow to	Run the feet of the tight end up the field—take on the pulling guard with the inside arm—force the play inside
Strong corner	Down—flow to	Secondary force
Weak corner	Scoop—flow away	Roll to post
Free safety	Down—run	Run alley to strongside

Wing T Wingback Counter (Figure 11-7)

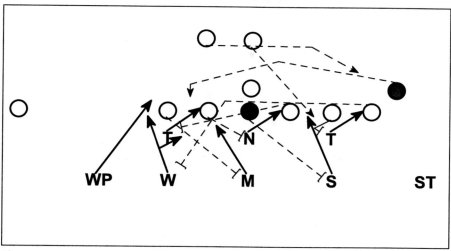

Figure 11-7

Position	Read	Fit
Strong tackle	Slant strong	Strong C gap
Weak tackle	Slant strong	Weak B gap
Nose	Slant strong	Strong A gap
Will	Down—flow to because of pull	Outside of the down block—may redirect under because of flow
Mike	Reach—flow weak because of pull	Fit under the down block by the tackle if possible—playside B gap
Sam	Scoop—flow away—because of pull	Backside A gap—take fullback
Whip	down—flow to	Run the feet of the tackle up the field—take on the pulling guard with the inside arm—force the play inside
Stud	Pull by tight end—away by wingback	Hold and fold
Strong corner	Down—flow to	Secondary force
Weak corner	Scoop—flow away	Roll to post
Free safety	Down—run	Run alley to strongside

Wing T Bootleg Keep (Figure 11-8)

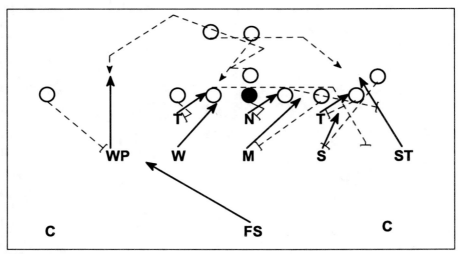

Figure 11-8

Position	Read	Fit
Strong tackle	Slant strong	Strong C gap
Weak tackle	Slant strong	Weak B gap
Nose	Slant strong	Strong A gap
Will	Scoop—flow away	Backside A gap—take fullback
Mike	Reach—flow strong	Fit under the down block by the tackle if possible—playside B gap
Sam	Down—flow to	Playside C gap—under the down block by the tight end or wingback
Whip	Scoop—flow away	Hold and fold—attack the quarterback as soon as he clears the mesh with the tailback
Stud	Down by tight end—flow to	Run the feet of the tight end up the field—take on the pulling guard with the inside arm—force the play inside
Strong corner	Down—flow to	Secondary force
Weak corner	Scoop—flow away	Roll to post
Free safety	Down—run	Run alley to strongside

12

Goal-Line Package and Defensive Special Teams

The 3-5-3 defense uses a very simple yet effective goal-line package. No matter where the ball is on the field, the goal-line package will not change. The goal-line front is designed to look and function as a double eagle front without having to rely on the outside linebackers to take on offensive linemen or a tight end man-to-man. Times will arise when you may choose to play the regular base front on the goal line and depend on pressure to accomplish what you are after.

*Front—*Goal line

Pressures

- All inside pressures can be called, but outside pressures are limited because of the alignment of the outside linebackers.
- If no specific pressure is called, then the goal-line call is automatically in Mike go.

  Coverages

- Cover 3 is used approximately 60 percent of the time on the goal line.
- Man coverage is used approximately 35 percent of the time on the goal line.
- Cover 1 is used the other 5 percent of the time.

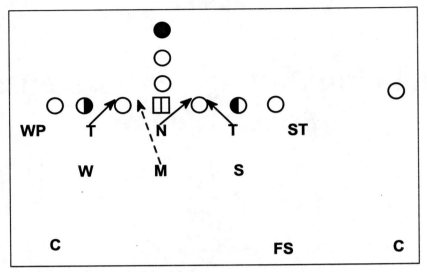

Figure 12-1. Versus double tight

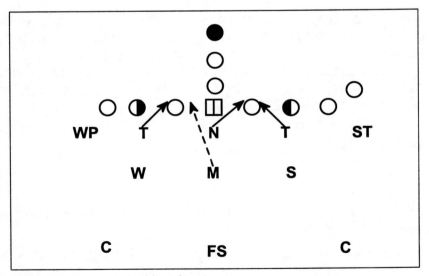

Figure 12-2. Versus double tight wing

Coverage Adjustments (Figures 12-3 through 12-8)

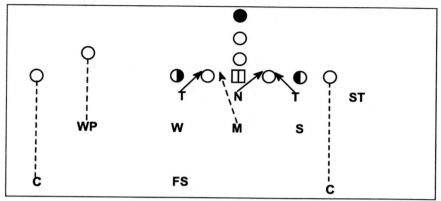

Figure 12-3. Goal line versus twins—Whip will be head up to number 2

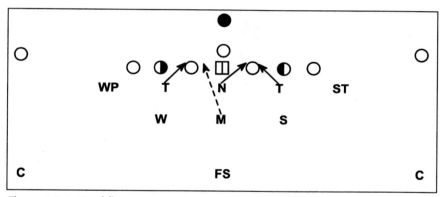

Figure 12-4. Goal line versus moose

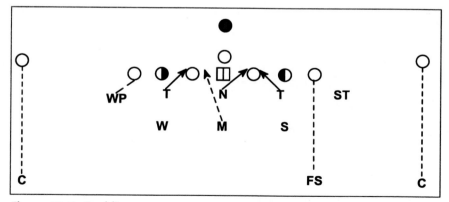

Figure 12-5. Goal line cover man versus moose

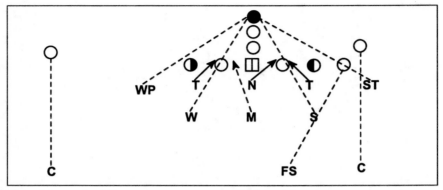
Figure 12-6. Goal line cover man versus double tight wing

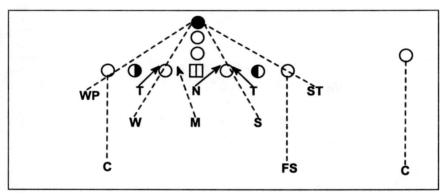
Figure 12-7. Goal line cover man versus double tight

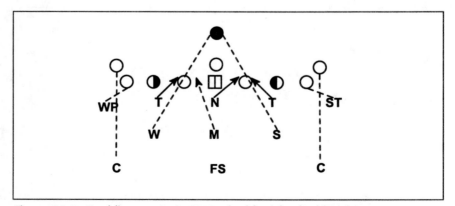
Figure 12-8. Goal line cover 1 versus double tight double wing

Defensive Special Teams

Punt Return/Rush

The punt return and punt rush assignments used with the 3-5-3 defense are quite simple, and usually require no substitutions except for a return man. The key point in good defensive special teams play is to always sell to the offense that you are sending the house to block the punt. Then, you can play games with different rushes and returns. Your opponent will have to spend a bunch of valuable practice time covering your special teams and not working on their own.

The punt rush team used in conjunction with the 3-5-3 involves numbering the defensive players, starting with the two players closest to the center (Figure 12-9). The nose will always align to the right and he is head up to the first man past the center. The Mike linebacker will be on the line of scrimmage and will always align to the left of the center. He is also head up to the first man past the center. Mike and the nose are both number 1. The two defensive tackles will align on the outside shoulder of the second men past the center to their side. They are both number 2. The Sam linebacker will always align to the right and will be on the outside shoulder of the third man past the center. The Will linebacker will be aligned like the Sam, but to the left of the center. Sam and Will are both number 3. The Stud linebacker will be aligned on the outside shoulder of the fourth man outside of the center and to the right. The Whip will be aligned like the Stud, but to the left. The Stud and Whip are number 4. Both corners will be aligned outside the Stud and Whip, unless they are called on to cover a receiver. The corners are number 5. The free safety will be removed and a return man will enter the game.

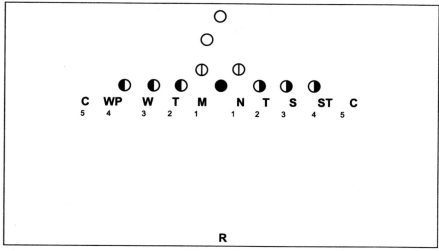

Figure 12-9. Numbering of defensive players

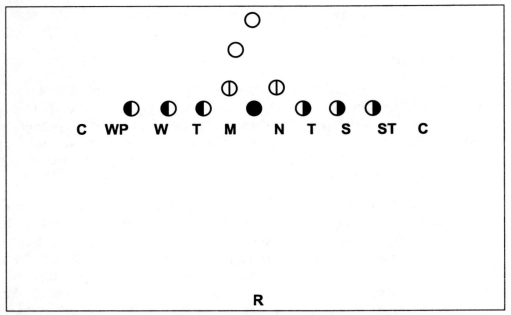

Figure 12-10. Punt return/rush versus tight punt

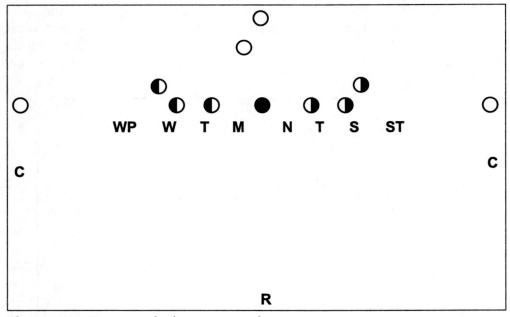

Figure 12-11. Punt return/rush versus spread punt

Assignments—Punt Rush

In the punt-rush phase of special teams play, the 3-5-3 defense will employ either an eight- or 10-man rush scheme. If a 10-man rush scheme is called for, the coach will simply signal for "block," usually by crossing his arms in front of his chest to form an X. If a 10-man rush is called, all 10 players on the line of scrimmage are trying to block the punt. A 10-man rush is illustrated in Figure 12-12 versus tight punt and in Figure 12-13 against spread punt.

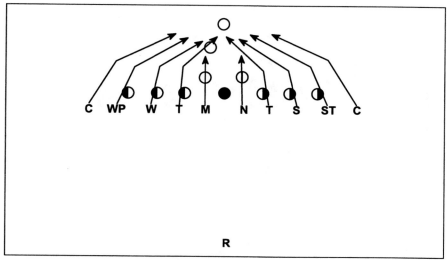

Figure 12-12. Block versus tight punt

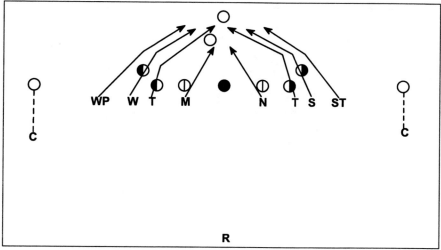

Figure 12-13. Block versus spread punt

If an eight-man rush is called, the coach will signal in a combination of numbers signifying which two players are stepping back and covering the two eligible receivers and watching for a fake. The coach can call 33, 44, 34, or 43. These numbers tell which players will stay. If 33 is called, then both number 3 players (Will and Sam) would fall back (Figure 12-14). If 44 is called, then the Stud and Whip would stay back (Figure 12-15). Next, if 34 is called, then the left number 3 and the right number 4 would stay (Figure 12-16). If 43 is called, then the left number 4 and the right number 3 would stay (Figure 12-17).

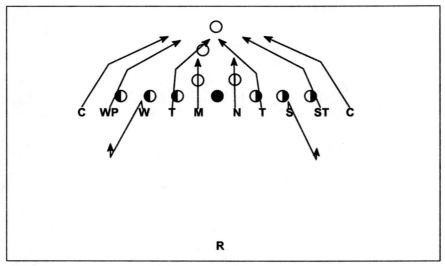

Figure 12-14. 33 call versus tight punt

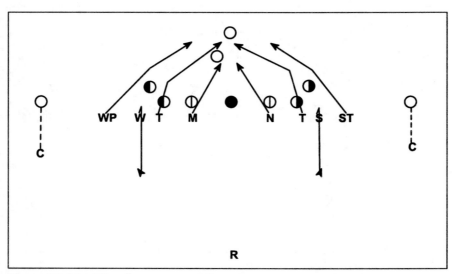

Figure 12-14a. 33 call versus spread punt

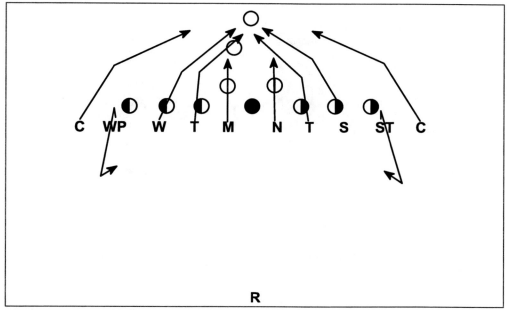

Figure 12-15. 44 call versus tight punt

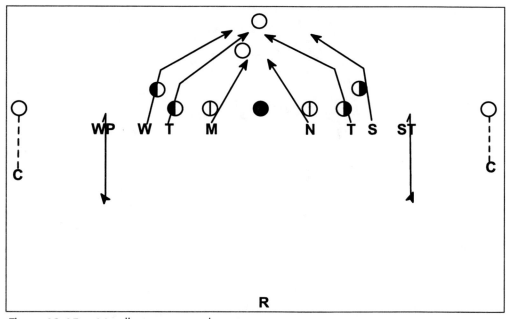

Figure 12-15a. 44 call versus spread punt

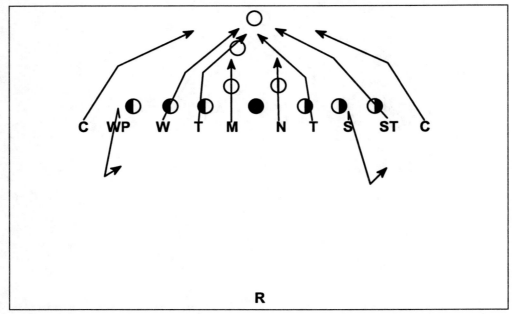

Figure 12-16. 43 call versus tight punt

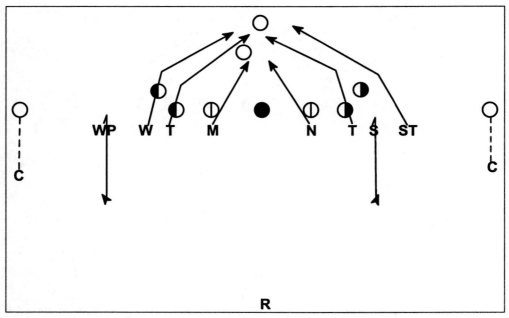

Figure 12-16a. 43 call versus spread punt

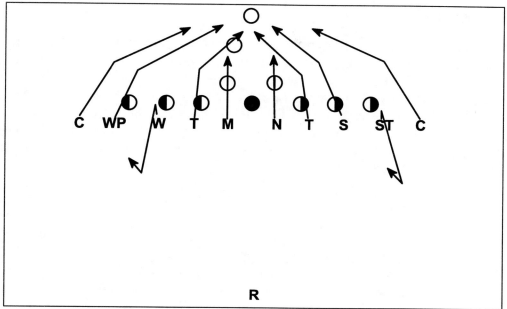

Figure 12-17. 34 call versus tight punt

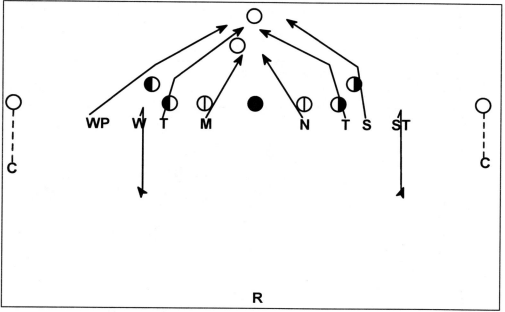

Figure 12-17a. 34 call versus spread punt

Assignments—Punt Return

The punt return will be used when the defense feels that gaining field position is more important than the possibility of a blocked punt. The punt return has the return side of the line stepping up the field and then peeling back downfield to set a wall. The Stud or Whip will take the wall to within 10 yards of the return man. The remaining players will space out five yards apart up the field. The players away from the call will rush as normal and then peel around and set a second wall across the field to the side called. Versus tight punt, the corners to both sides rush and make sure the ball is kicked before peeling back and helping out with a block downfield.

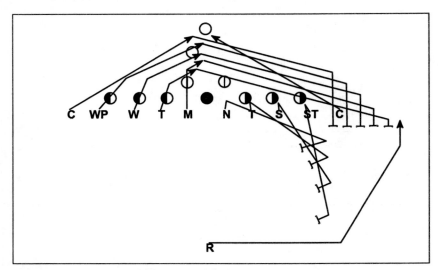

Figure 12-18. Return right versus tight punt

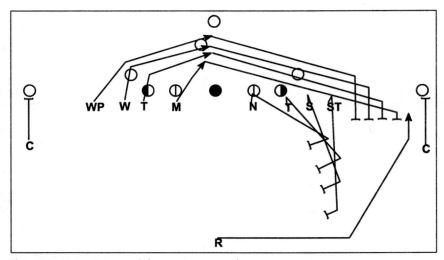

Figure 12-18a. Return right versus spread punt

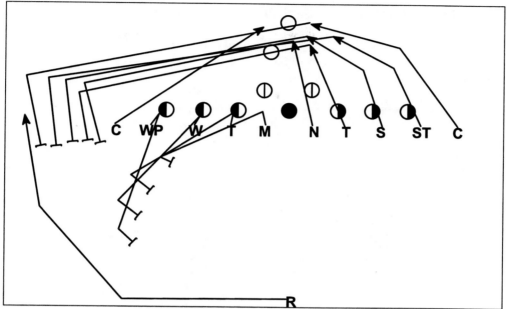

Figure 12-19. Return left versus tight punt

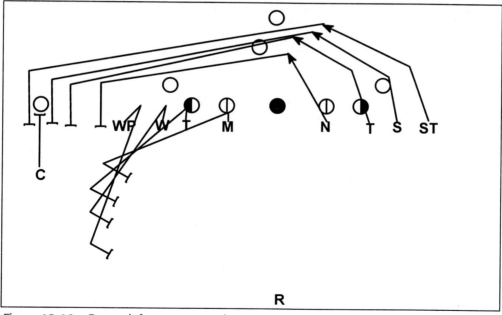

Figure 12-19a. Return left versus spread punt

Point After Touchdown/Field Goal Block (Figure 12-20)

The same set of alignments and rush rules will be used for the point after touchdown/field goal block as are used for the punt block. The possible calls that can be made are "block," 33, 44, 34, and 43.

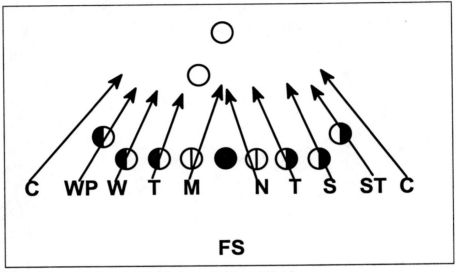

Figure 12-20. Point after touchdown/field goal block

A

Defensive Practice Schedule

Two-Platoon Team

Period	Time	Activity	Notes
1	4:00	Flex	Entire team
2	4:05	Flex	
3	4:10	Special teams	Entire team
4	4:15	Special teams	
5	4:20	Special teams	
6	4:25	Special teams	
7	4:30	Individual	
8	4:35	Individual	
9	4:40	Individual	
10	4:45	Individual	
11	4:50	Individual	Outside linebackers with defensive backs for
12	4:55	Individual	man-coverage drills
13	5:00	Individual	Defensive line and inside linebackers blitz drill
14	5:05	Inside	
15	5:10	Inside	Defensive line and inside linebackers
16	5:15	Inside	
17	5:20	Skeleton	
18	5:25	Skeleton	Inside/outside linebackers and defensive backs
19	5:30	Skeleton	
20	5:35	Team	Entire team
21	5:40	Team	1 versus 2—periods 20–22
22	5:45	Team	2 versus 1—periods 23–25
23	5:50	Team	Goal line mixed into script
24	5:55	Team	
25	6:00	Team	
26	6:05	Conditioning	Entire team
27	6:10	Conditioning	

Single-Platoon Team

Period	Time	Activity	Notes
1	4:00	Flex	Entire team
2	4:05	Flex	
3	4:10	Special teams	
4	4:15	Special teams	Entire team
5	4:20	Special teams	
6	4:25	Offensive individual	
7	4:30	Offensive individual	
8	4:35	Offensive Individual	
9	4:40	Offensive inside	
10	4:45	Offensive inside	
11	4:50	Offensive skeleton	
12	4:55	Offensive skeleton	
13	5:00	Offensive team	
14	5:05	Offensive team	
15	5:10	Offensive team	
16	5:15	Defensive individual	
17	5:20	Defensive individual	
18	5:25	Defensive individual	
19	5:30	Defensive inside	
20	5:35	Defensive inside	
21	5:40	Defensive skeleton	
22	5:45	Defensive skeleton	
23	5:50	Defensive team	
24	5:55	Defensive team	
25	6:00	Defensive team	
26	6:05	Conditioning	Entire team
27	6:10	Conditioning	

B

Installation Schedule

Practice	Team	Defensive Line	Inside Linebackers	Outside Linebackers	Defensive Backs
1	Base	Slant strong	Go, Mike/Sam/Will 3	Fire, Whip/Stud 3	3
2	Base	Slant weak	Go, Mike/Sam/Will 3	Fire, Whip/ Stud 3	3
3	Base	In	Dog, strong/weak 3	A, Whip/Stud/Double 3	3
4	Tuff	Out	Dog, strong/weak	A, Whip/Stud/Double Man	Man
5	Tuff	Pinch	Wash	Wash Man	Man
6	Goal line	Review	Wash	Wash Man	Man
7	Goal line	Review	Smash	Smash 1	1
8	Jett	Review	Smash	Smash 1	1
9	Jett	Review	Bat	1	1
10	Review	Review	Bat	4	4
11	Review	Review	Review	4	4
12	Review	Review	Review	4	4
13	Review	Review	Review	Sky	Sky
14	Review	Review	Review	Sky	Sky
15	Review	Review	Review	Sky	Sky

About the Author

Thomas Cousins is the head coach at Avon Park High School in Avon Park, Florida, where he also serves as the offensive coordinator and quarterbacks coach. He has been a part of the Avon Park High School football coaching staff since 1999 and has been the head coach since 2003.

Cousins has been involved with the game of football for more than 30 years as either a player or coach. He began his coaching career at Newberry College, from which he graduated with an English degree in 1992, and then made stops at Goose Creek High School in Goose Creek, South Carolina, Charleston Southern University in Charleston, South Carolina, and Hardee High School in Wauchula, Florida.

Cousins is also an active lecturer at football clinics around the country.

He and his wife, Danna, have two children, Jeffrey and Haley.